Texans One and All

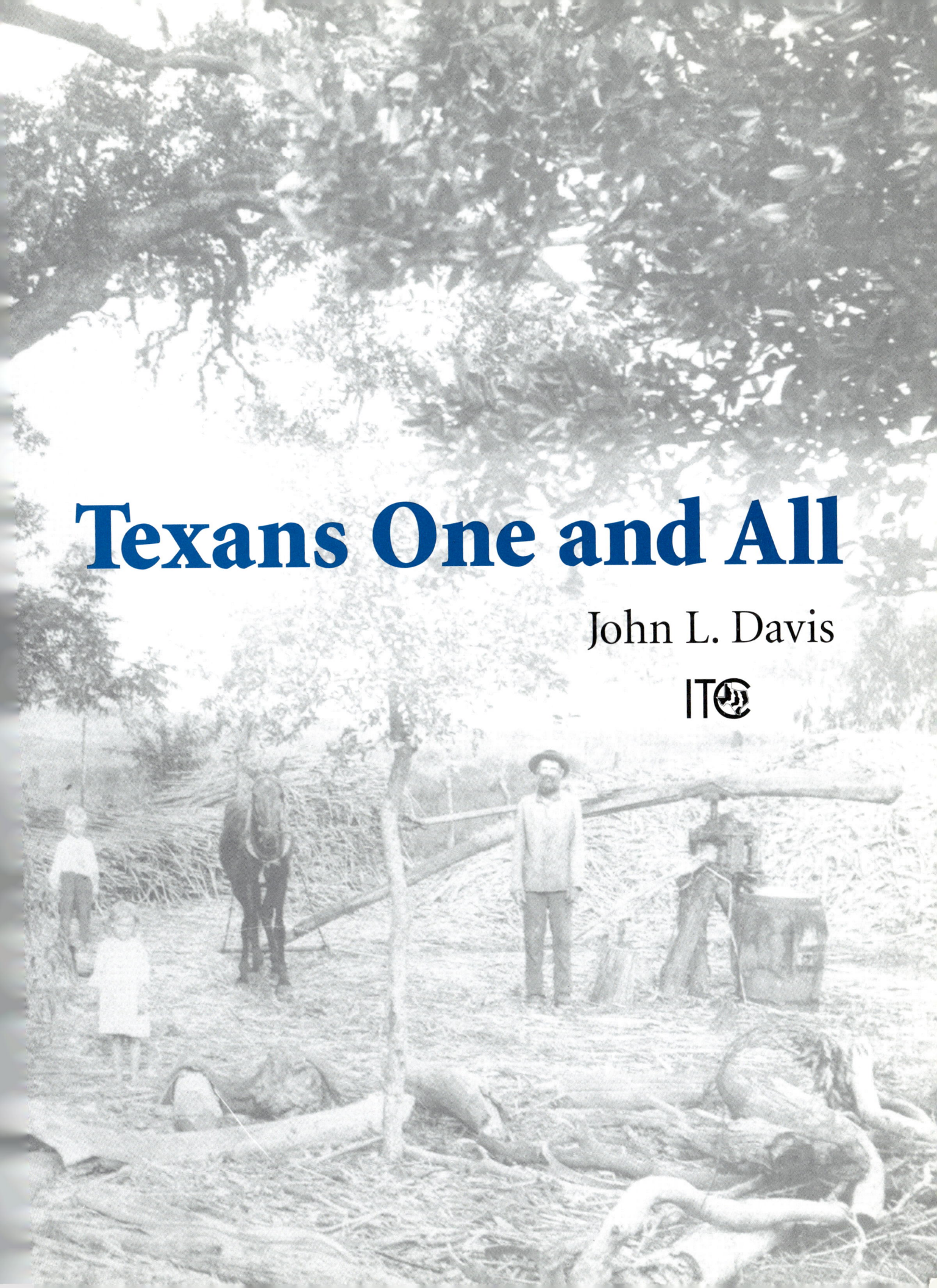
Texans One and All

John L. Davis

ITC

> The Institute of Texan Cultures is a university educational center dedicated to enhancing the understanding of the history and diverse cultures of Texas through exhibits, programs, and publications that encourage acceptance and appreciation of our differences as well as our common humanity. Operating on the premise that people are stronger citizens when they know more about themselves and each other, the Institute provides a forum for understanding culture and history and symbolizes the state's strength in diversity.
>
> —*ITC Mission Statement*

EDITOR'S NOTE: There is really no one way more logical than another to order the ethnic groups represented on the ITC Exhibit Floor and portrayed here, so we have chosen to put them in the order in which they appear on the Exhibit Floor as of the production of this book, Winter 1998, beginning with the Native American and moving clockwise around to the Tejano Area.

The Exhibit Floor is an ever-changing stage, however, on which we tell the stories of the peoples of Texas; as those stories change and additions are made and public interests vary, so may the order of the exhibits to some extent. Therefore, it may be that, on a visit, you notice some differences between the actual Exhibit Floor arrangement and this book; attribute them to Progress!

Texans One and All
by John L. Davis

©1998 The University of Texas Institute of Texan Cultures at San Antonio
801 South Bowie Street, San Antonio, Texas 78205-3296

Rex H. Ball, Executive Director

Lynn J. Catalina, Director of Communications and Project Director

Laurie Gudzikowski, Project Adviser

Mary Lou Ellis, Director of Production

Production Staff: Sandra Hodsdon Carr, editor and designer; Tom Shelton, photo archivist; Allee Wallace and Laura Howard, photographic lab work; Jim Cosgrove, graphic adviser and back cover illustrator

International Standard Book Number 0-86701-074-6

Photo on title pages—*The (Polish) John Dugosh family making molasses in Bandera, c. 1910*

Printed in the United States of America

Contents

Introduction	viii
The Exhibit Floor	x
The Flags of Texas Settlers	xiv
Texans One and All:	
The Native American Texans	2
The Anglo-American Texans	6
The English Texans	10
The Hungarian Texans	12
The Scottish Texans	14
The Irish Texans	16
The Danish Texans	18
The Norwegian Texans	20
The Swedish Texans	22
The African-American Texans	24
The Jewish Texans	28
The Swiss Texans	30
The German Texans	32
The Wendish Texans	36
The Czech Texans	38
The Polish Texans	40
The Italian Texans	42
The Japanese Texans	44
The Chinese Texans	46
The Dutch Texans	48
The Belgian Texans	50
The Greek Texans	52
The Filipino Texans	54
The French Texans	56
The Lebanese and Syrian Texans	58
The Tejanos	60
ITC Product Information	64
Photo Credits	66

Introduction

The Institute of Texan Cultures was formed as the exhibit of the State of Texas at HemisFair '68, the world's fair held in San Antonio. Simultaneously, ITC was defined as a permanent research and production center dealing with the history of the peoples who make up Texas.

The Institute's charge as an educational center has not changed. And the peoples of Texas remain fascinating and complex. Texas is, of course, a land, a state, once a nation, a huge and mixed ecology, a ritual happening, a stereotype, an economy, a state of mind, a way of life—and *people*.

The land is huge and varied—with more than 30,000 years of immigrant history—and remains one of the remarkable crossroads of the world. Here are individuals, families, and settlements representing every major cultural, geographic, ethnic, and political group in the world...and nearly all smaller groups as well.

Change has always been a part of Texan cultures. Groups have blended with others, leaving hardly a trace; others maintain a strong identity. All groups are immigrants, and the group arriving today changes, or is changed by, other arrivals. This process has created understanding, tolerance, and enjoyment as well as occasional misunderstanding, unease, and outright hate. Some cultural traits have been honored among all peoples; some customs have been insulted and destroyed.

As a vast generalization, native groups came to Texas first, hardly as a single culture but as settlement waves displacing each other as living patterns changed for more than 200 centuries. European colonization, since the start of the 16th century, shifted dominance to Spanish, then Mexican, rule and settlement.

In the early 19th century, Anglo-American immigrants (predominantly descendants of northern Europeans) re-created Texas in their image quickly—and enduring to the present time.

Hill Country ranch

And in all years in settlements large and small, individuals and families, freedmen and slaves, legal and illegal arrivals came to make a new home. Texas attracted investors and cattle raisers, miners and lumbermen, cotton growers and stonemasons, homemakers and teachers, criminals and ministers...women and men in every category. And they came from everywhere in the world.

The population of Texas consists of people from a hundred origins from Afghan to Zambian, "native" to "foreign-born," "unknown" to "born at sea." But they are Texans—one and all.

Where groups or communities exist, they always change in number and in way of life—and occasionally in preferred name. In this there is nothing unique. People have often moved to new, more empty lands to find a future. Some run from old troubles, and a few simply need new horizons.

In Texas this complex settlement history bloomed with heroism, sacrifice, creativity, and excitement. It is laced with a fair supply of wild stories and extremes: treasures and ghosts, brutality and kindness, failure and success.

The mission of the Institute of Texan Cultures is to tell these stories through permanent and traveling exhibits, publications, audiovisuals, curricula, interpretive programs, and public events including concerts, symposia, and the Texas Folklife Festival.

Twenty-six exhibit areas at ITC are outlined in this publication. A few, only a very few, questions are answered: What are the major settlement groups in Texas? Where did these people choose to live? Why did they come and when? What's a good story about... ? This book is a portrait and maybe a souvenir. But it is only a beginning to the stories.

What is mentioned here is expanded in the exhibits and productions of ITC, but only somewhat. One must, to know Texas, look at Texans one and all.

The Exhibit Floor

The Exhibit Floor of the Institute of Texan Cultures, street level of a three-story building, is designed as the main public display area.

On this multiple-use floor—in an area the size of a football field—are 26 exhibits representing the ethnic and cultural groups of Texas, five interpretive areas, and an audiovisual presentation on a multiple-screen dome 90 feet in diameter.

Here are several thousand photographs and paintings and text panels and murals dealing with 30,000 years of Texas history. And on this Exhibit Floor are the sledgehammers, musical instruments, sewing paraphernalia, shirts and blouses, doctor's bags, looms, tipis, branding irons, pottery, hearses, plows, kettles, religious icons, ceremonial dragons, sacred books, drawings, rifles, bayonets, bonnets, barbed wire, quilts, games, cannons, combs, coins, cotton bales, diaries, foods, herbs, notebooks, earrings, menorahs, tractors, arrow points, chispas, trunks and kyrkasks, and one snuslåda...most everything that went—and still goes—into making a life by the people who made Texas.

This display area contains an entire house (a sharecropper's home), a German bandstand, American Indian dwellings and camps (from three areas of Texas), a two-ton Panhandle tractor, miniature dioramas of San Antonio's Main Plaza and a 1790s Spanish Colonial home, a log-skidder from East Texas with wheels eight feet in diameter, and a six-foot-diameter world globe next to a ten-foot relief map of Texas for orientation.

Orientation is necessary. The displays are often called overwhelming in detail. This museum contains enough texts, maps, photographs, and engravings to fill many books.

But also on the Exhibit Floor are docents who will answer questions. At various places among the exhibits are interpretive

The globe with part of the Texas map on the left

areas of special interest to visitors who want an explanation and a demonstration.

The Plains Indian section of the Native American Area

The interpretive areas include a puppet theater where Texas history is dramatized for the very young; a chuck wagon where one can see and hear the importance of food preparation to, and a lot more about, the cattle drives that were a dramatic part of Texas history; a fibers and fabrics area where the history of cotton, wool, and mohair lives in actual demonstration; a *jacal*, home of many early Texas settlers, where one can see corn ground the old way; a typical 1970s Tejano living room; and a post office. The post office, brought from Geronimo, Texas, is a working office, where a docent sells stamps and spins a few stories. A visitor can mail a card here to be stamped with the ITC postmark.

In these interpretive areas, researchers and docents with first-hand expertise talk to tour groups or—in quieter moments—to individuals. The visitor to the Institute who asks a question of a staff member may be in for quite a conversation.

Guided tours for organized groups and school classes are available in many flavors and topics, including an overview of Texas settlement, what goes on in Texas today, methods of transportation, and the languages of the state.

Using the audiovisual dome area and making temporary changes, the Institute staff has turned the main Exhibit Floor into the site of live television shows, film productions, and large special displays. Thematic exhibits such as the history of aviation in Texas and the archaeologically restored remains of Spanish shipwrecks from the Texas coast have covered over a quarter of the Exhibit Floor.

The cultural exhibits, each centering on one of Texas's peoples, range from 50 to 10 feet in diameter. Changes and alterations in the exhibits have been carried out in every year of Institute

Part of the Belgian Area

xi

A view of the Colonial Roots section of the Tejano Area

Grinding corn at the jacal in the Tejano Area

operation, from bringing in a single artifact to the addition of new exhibit areas. Future plans include creation of topical exhibit areas showing the wonderful and obvious similarities between people. Ongoing research will reflect changes in how people perceive themselves and will highlight very recent arrivals. Time changes all.

Additional display spaces at ITC include an Upper Gallery near the main entrance, which often features thematic exhibits from the Institute's three-million-image photographic collection. Most of the images on the Exhibit Floor are housed in the Institute's library collections and have been assembled from professional collections, copied during Photo Heritage Days held in a number of towns in Central and South Texas, and borrowed from thousands of individuals across the state.

This book contains photographs of people, places, and artifacts from the museum floor, from former displays, and from collections not yet used in exhibits.

The Lower Gallery, downstairs from the Exhibit Floor, hosts shows from other museums and research institutions or displays the traveling and special exhibits produced by the Institute itself. Gallery exhibits have included retrospectives of the works of Texas artists; a history of fine book publication in Texas; displays of Mexican textiles and masks; an exhibit of Texas quiltmaking; the not-quite tongue-in-cheek "What Is a Texan?" exhibit; a photographic history of landscape changes; the demographics of Texas; a magnificent collection of African-American art; a detailed look at urban change; the story of exploration in the Southwest; Texas music; and Texas foods.

Outside the Institute building is an interpretive area known as the "Back 40."

The term itself is unofficial and is simply a phrase farmers have used for the 40-acre plot, or whatever-size field, lying some distance from the main house or barn. The area is in back of the Institute building but, far from being remote, is one of the most interactive exhibit areas.

The plan for the area has been to replicate typical Texas buildings at either full or slightly reduced scale: a loft barn, a one-room schoolhouse, a high-plains windmill, an 1870s frontier military fort barracks, an adobe home, a brush arbor, and a two-room dogtrot log house.

Many of the furnishings in this area—school desks and books, farm tools, wagons, cupboards, lanterns, chairs—can be sat in, handled, hefted, and smelled. Institute staff members and docents offer guided tours and special programs inside and outside the buildings.

Visiting the Back 40 is not quite like being young in a hot, one-room schoolhouse or working in a Hill Country barn on a Spring day or living in the cool enclosure of thick adobe walls. In today's frenetic world, it's hard to daydream of simpler times, harder still to really understand what frontier life was like. This is the place to come close to that experience.

The bandstand in the German Area

A view of the Back 40 showing the log house, the Hill Country barn, the Eclipse windmill, the schoolhouse, and the adobe house in the distance

xiii

The Flags of Texas Settlers

Most of the flags displayed in front of the Institute were in use when the peoples of their respective nations first came to Texas.

At least, this was the original idea. However, some individuals and groups departed their native countries long before a national flag was adopted; some left areas that had no "flag" in the European sense of the word; some peoples coming to Texas did not want to be represented by a hated symbol; and some groups emigrated from countries in which the national standard was disputed.

The Texas flag represents all peoples, every ethnic and cultural group in the state.

Lone Star: This familiar flag was adopted by the Third Congress of the Republic of Texas meeting in Houston on January 25, 1839. At the time, some five other popular designs were either in use or had been suggested for adoption.

Belgium: The national flag of Belgium was adopted in 1830. The colors—black, yellow, and red—are from the coat of arms of the House of Brabant.

China: The Manchu dragon flag of Imperial China was adopted in 1872. Originally triangular with a blue dragon and red sun on a yellow field, the flag was altered to a rectangular shape in 1890.

Czech Republic: When Czechs began coming to Texas, there was no Czech Republic. The national flag was adopted in 1920. Red and white are colors of the historic kingdom of Bohemia; blue represents the province of Moravia.

Denmark: The national flag of Denmark has been used since 1219, when Denmark virtually ruled the Baltic. By legend, the flag descended from heaven during a military siege. Never changed, it is the oldest flag still in use without alteration.

England: St. George is the patron saint of England. St. George's flag became England's national symbol in 1277.

France: A white flag became the royal ensign when Henry III came to the throne in 1574. In the subsequent reign of Henry IV, it became the symbol of the French Bourbons. On occasion, the pure white flag was used as a naval flag but was not favored because of the connotation of surrender.

Germany: Three German state and province flags are flown. At the time of the first significant German
Hesse settlement in Texas, there was no unified Germany. The flags of **Hesse**, **Mecklenburg**, and
Mecklenburg **Saxony** represent the variety of German flags in use before the founding of the German
Saxony Empire in 1871.

Greece: The Greek national flag dates from 1832, when the country won independence from Turkey.

Ireland: Although Ireland did not become an independent nation until 1922, the color combination of the modern Irish flag was in use in 1848.

Italy: The Italian naval flag symbolizes the period of Italian immigration to America.

Japan: The Japanese national flag came into use in 1870. The sun, traditional ancestor of the emperor, has been used on Japanese flags for more than a thousand years.

Lebanon: Lebanese immigrants, often identified as Syrians, began coming to Texas long before their country became independent. The cedar tree is the national symbol of Lebanon.

Mexico: The Mexican state flag was adopted in virtually its present form in 1833. The Mexican coat of arms, an eagle on a cactus with a serpent in its beak, denotes the founding of Tenochtitlán, capital city of the Aztec empire.

Netherlands: The Netherlands flag dates from the Dutch revolt against Spanish rule led by William of Orange. It was adopted in 1579 and changed in 1630 to the version flown.

Norway: The Norwegian national flag was first introduced as the Norwegian merchant flag in 1821.

Poland: The flag of the dependent Russian Kingdom of Poland came into being after the Napoleonic Wars. The blue cross denotes Russian rule of Poland; the Polish eagle is the national symbol.

Scotland: St. Andrew is the patron saint of Scotland. His cross appears on Scotland's national flag, also called St. Andrew's flag.

Spain: The flag of Castile and León was the first national flag of Spain. It was the flag carried by Christopher Columbus in 1492.

Sweden: The Swedish national flag, a yellow cross on a blue field, has been flown since 1523.

Switzerland: The white cross on red was carried by Swiss soldiers as early as 1339. The flag was adopted as the national flag in 1848. The square version was established in 1889.

United States: The flag flown commemorates those who came to Texas from the United States. It is the flag of 1820 bearing 23 stars and 13 stripes. This flag was in use when American settlers first came to Texas in 1821.

When the flags were first flown at the opening of the Institute of Texan Cultures in 1968, nearly every design was considered correct and approved for display by either a national consulate or embassy located in the United States. Some nations, China, for instance, could not then be asked; some nations no longer existed in an older form—Italy, for example. A few nations, such as Scotland, had been long conquered by others and necessarily regarded their flag as of historic moment. And the Native Americans had a host of banners and standards reminiscent of the Roman Empire, but they were not unified symbols. At the time of the original research, ambassadors from some nations requested that an earlier version of a flag not be displayed. For these groups, other representative flags are flown. Further, initial research at the Institute did not complete study of a few research topics, e.g., Russian settlement, Gypsy migrations, and Wendish origins; thus, certain problems were avoided by omission.

In the Anglo-American section of the Institute's main floor is an exhibit displaying 43 of the flags used in Texas at one time or another.

In any case, flags are national symbols evoking strong feelings, both good and bad. They are flown here in honor of the peoples who made Texas. The back cover shows the flags of ITC in color.

Haymarket Plaza, San Antonio, c. 1925

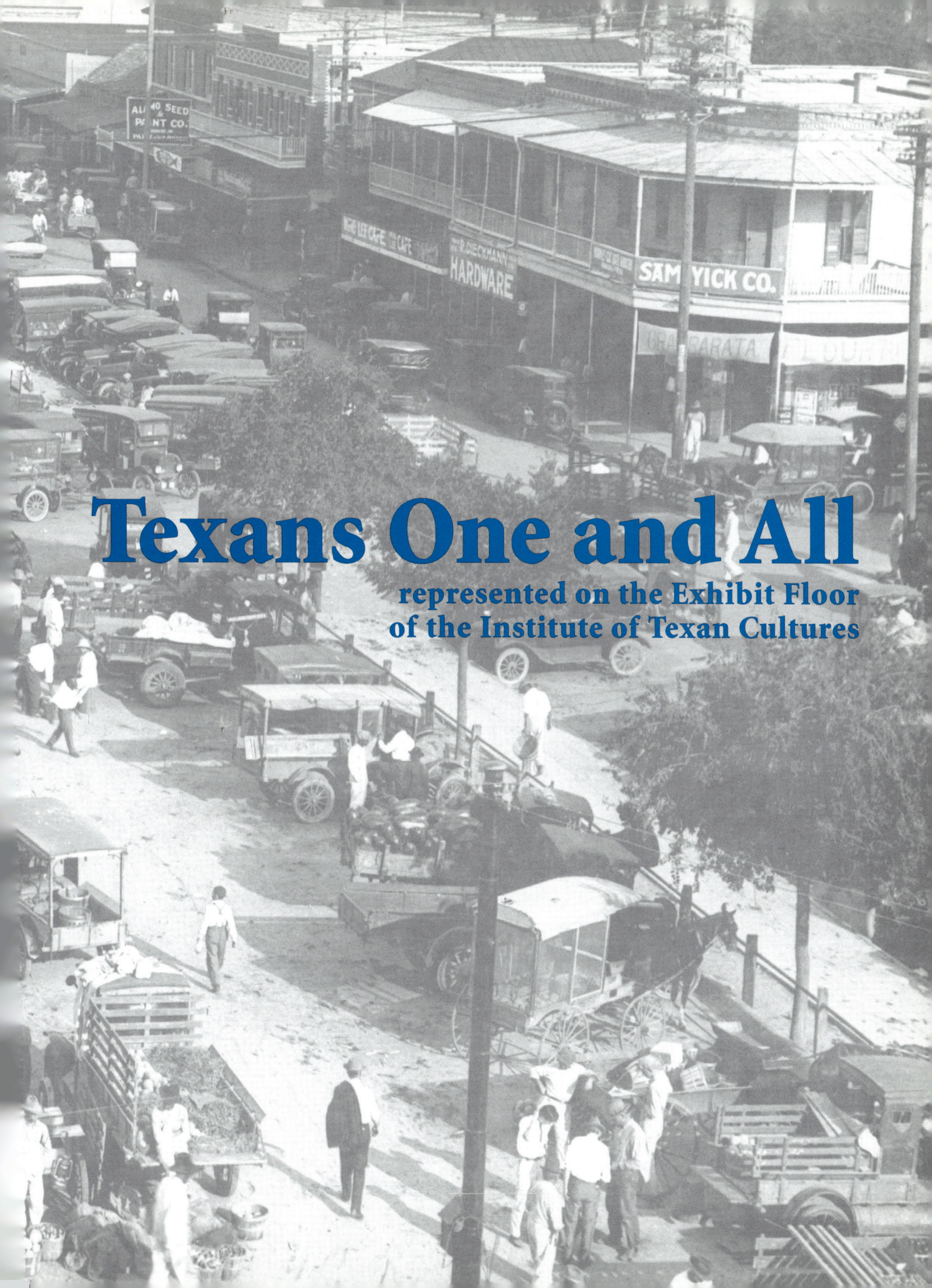

Texans One and All
represented on the Exhibit Floor of the Institute of Texan Cultures

The Native American Texans

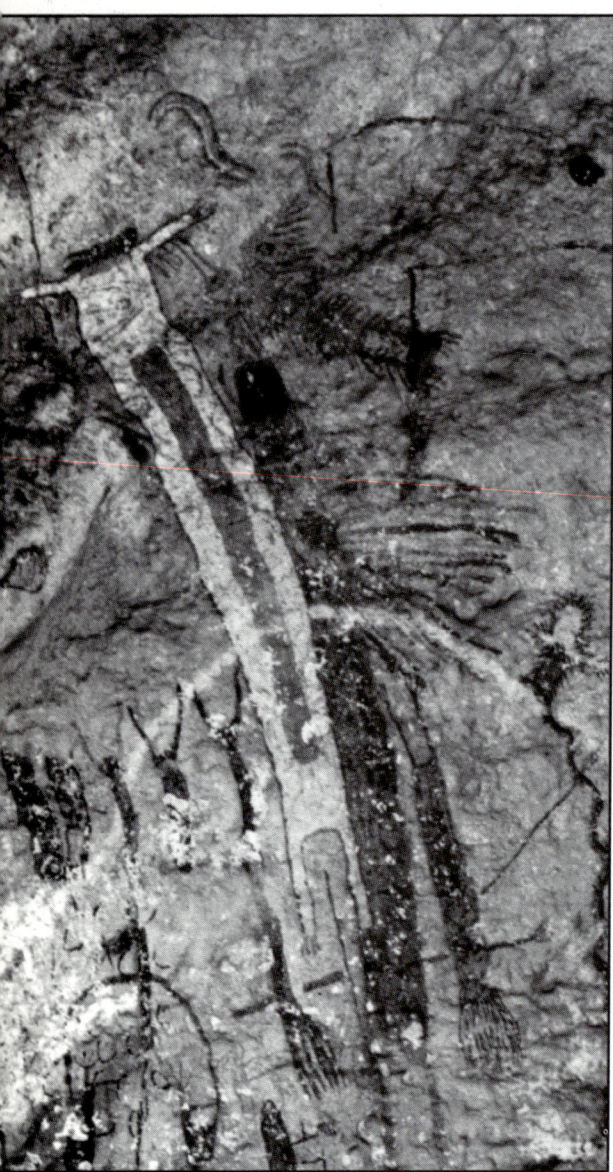

The "White Shaman," an Archaic-period pictograph from the Lower Pecos River area

Reconstruction of an ancient Caddo dwelling in Caddoan Mounds State Historical Park

Native American history is the story of one of the most complex and violent cultural changes in North America. Native Americans are people descended from the first humans who migrated from Asia to North America, arriving on the continent by perhaps 30,000 years ago. Direct evidence places them in Texas some 12,000 years before the present.

Europeans, discovering the huge linked continents of North and South America, called the natives by several names. Christopher Columbus used the name "Indians" to support the rigorously held idea that he had found parts of Asia, perhaps the East Indies. This name stuck.

European and United States history, government reports, and narrative fiction has, until recent times, spoken of "Indians," "Indian affairs," or "natives." The latter term is now accepted by many of the people themselves.

Native Americans are not and never were a single culture; they were much more diverse than the peoples of Europe.

The early natives passed on their stories and traditions orally and through such means as rock art. Recorded historical accounts of Native Americans have been interpreted by anthropologists and archaeologists in contemporary times and not usually by the natives themselves.

More is known about some cultures than about others; certain regions of Texas such as the lower Pecos and the trans-Pecos provide more to the story because of well-preserved artifacts such as potsherds, sandals, arrow points, scrapers, needles, ornaments, basket shreds, grinding stones, and even the bones of the people themselves. Other areas provide fewer clues. Still, much is known.

The actual number of Indians in the Texas area was never great, estimated at 45,000 before written history to only a few thousand in the mid-19th century.

In Texas at least four cultural areas of the Indian met and, to some degree, blended: Western Gulf, Southeast, Southwest, and Plains. Within these huge categories defined by Europeans were groups with wide variety in cultural patterns and languages. All were linked by trade and competition, commonalities and conflicts. They were as diverse as the lands they occupied.

The groups, called bands or tribes by Europeans, were known by names which were approximations of what the people called themselves or, on occasion, location names transliterated into Spanish and French and English.

Indians of the Western Gulf—northeastern Mexico and the Texas coastal plains south of San Antonio—were people who hunted and foraged for a living. . .as far as we know. Men wore little or no clothing much of the year; women wore simple skirts of buckskin. Homes were small domes of bent saplings or cane with skin or woven covers. Their possessions—tools, containers, storage vessels, bedding, weapons, packs, toys—seem to have been minimal.

Fish and game animals provided food, supplemented by wild plants. Along the coast these people were known as the Karankawas and were perhaps the first natives encountered by the

Spanish in present Texas. Other nomadic groups, called Coahuiltecans by Europeans, lived inland to the west and north as far as present San Antonio.

The cultural area of Southeastern natives stretched from the Atlantic Coast past the Trinity River in Texas. The Caddos and Atakapans were the most numerous in that area. From the Caddos Spanish explorers recorded a word perhaps pronounced "tayshas," which referred to friends or allies. The Spanish made reference to "los Texas" and probably first used the word as an area name.

The Caddos had the most complex culture of Texas natives, although their civilization was in decline even before the arrival of Europeans. They built efficient and durable wood-framed, thatched homes and ceremonial centers, constructed impressive burial mounds, and created professional work areas. They were farmers with ranked social orders and elaborate belief systems.

Not a lot is known about the natives of the present trans-Pecos area. They were certainly on the edge of the influence of the huge Southwest Pueblo centers. Most lived near rivers and farmed; some built one-story thatched mud-and-river-cane buildings. Their crops of beans, corn, peppers, and squash were adopted by the Spanish. More is known about the peoples of the lower Pecos, who lived in dry rock shelters, which helped in the preservation over the centuries of their belongings.

Yet, group names in the West remain uncertain. For one reason, the Spanish did not explore the area in detail and often applied the same name to different groups. The word "Jumano," for example, referred to several groups in Texas's trans-Pecos and in Arizona and New Mexico. One Jumano group in Texas hunted buffalo on the Southern Plains and was Plains Indian in nature. Another Jumano group—or the same people at different times—lived in a cluster of villages centered on the confluence of the Rio Grande and Rio Concho and was distantly Puebloan in culture.

Quanah Parker, Comanche leader and son of Chief Peta Nocoma and white captive Cynthia Ann Parker, was one of the last warriors to accept defeat by the U.S. Army and surrender at Ft. Sill.

Comanche family at Ft. Sill

Although the Spanish were wide-ranging enough not to stereotype the natives, except as natives, Plains Indians became "The Indians" to many Anglo-American Texans.

Plains cultures extended fully across the Llano Estacado and Edwards Plateau...and into other areas when the Plains Indians wished. These groups, including Apaches, Kiowas, Kiowa-Apaches, Comanches, Wichitas, and Tonkawas, were hunters and warriors by way of life and reputation.

These groups, having acquired horses and firearms, became mounted warrior societies. For a time, they excelled against both Europeans and other native groups. Although some bands did farm, most were highly mobile and very dependent on the main natural resource—buffalo. Not always friendly among themselves, intertribal warfare changed their boundaries often. But the main pressure to move came from Spanish settlement to the south and Anglo occupation from the east.

Thus, overlapping native cultures of the Plains were driven together and displaced, often shifted more than a thousand miles. With the arrival of the Spanish and, later, the relatively immense number of Anglo-American settlers, the native story changes to one of reaction. European settlement, intentionally and unintentionally, literally exterminated native cultures. "European settlement" meant land ownership, more efficient forms of farming and hunting, large numbers of people, the introduction of new, often

Kickapoo family in Nacimiento, Coahuila, Mexico, c. 1900

fatal diseases, and the ability to use technology and religion to their advantage in attempts to usurp the land—backed by the cavalry and Texas Rangers. Indians were neither technologically equipped nor numerous enough to oppose the Europeans. They tried.

The Spanish, never as effective as Anglos against Indians in a military sense, nevertheless brought in the mission system in an attempt to alter native cultures. To some degree, this succeeded. Anglos were more pure conquerors who pushed the Indians out or killed them. Many exceptions exist; the generality was the rule.

From the early 19th century, Texas became a crossroads for Indians as well as Europeans. Tribal groups and shattered remnants of cultures crossed the land: Cheyennes, Osages, Pawnees, Kickapoos, Navajos, Pueblos, Apaches, Choctaws, Chickasaws, Creeks, Cherokees, Delawares, Shawnees, Biloxis, Quapaws, Yaquis, mixed heritages such as the black Seminoles, and scores of others.

Texas became a battlefield many a time—not always native versus European—but, during the Mexican and Civil Wars and in the late 19th century, Indian raids against the newcomers became almost common. To settlers on a night of the Comanche Moon, the western frontier was as close as ten miles west of Austin. With firearms and the horse, the Plains Indians, in particular, became formidable. But, ultimately, the struggle was one-sided.

Texas set up reserves for a short time, reservations under state jurisdiction because Texas retained all public land when joining the United States as an independent nation. The desirability of the land soon brought the effort to an end. Natives who remained in Texas were taken into Indian Territory (future Oklahoma), driven into northern Mexico, or killed. A few adopted a profile low enough for survival. Fewer still served as Army scouts and Ranger guides, but their allegiance made little difference in the long run.

Three small groups stayed in Texas, at first on private land, then on donated or purchased land later expanded into "reservations." None originally lived in the area of modern Texas. Fragments of Alabama and Coushatta groups still live near Woodville, and a group of Tiguas lives southeast of downtown El Paso in Ysleta.

Black Seminole Scouts at Ft. Clark, c. 1885: (from left) unidentified man, Billy July, Ben July, Denbo Factor, Ben Wilson, John July, and William Shields. Descendants of the July family still live in Southwest Texas.

The latter are descendants of Pueblos who followed the Spaniards south from New Mexico three centuries ago. These groups have a strong tribal organization and welcome tourists to displays, activities, and museums. Recently, remnants of the Kickapoo tribe have been recognized as a native group and have been granted land near the Rio Grande at El Indio.

Other dispersed groups and descendants remain in Texas, a few trying to carry on the traditions of their ancestors: black Seminoles can still be found, especially in South Texas; some Cherokees live in rural East Texas, descendants of those few who successfully hid for several generations; Caddos also live in East Texas; and Yaquis still live on both sides of the Rio Grande since an earlier deportation from northwestern Mexico.

In modern times the Federal Bureau of Indian Affairs brought Indians from all over the continent to Dallas, Houston, and San Antonio. Programs of the Field Employment Assistance Office, now discarded, placed them in urban centers with the goal of their entering the world that had surrounded them.

In Texas today some 18,000 people are listed as Native American; many of these are not "native" to the immediate area. Perhaps 200,000 claim mixed blood. Earlier, few individuals would admit to mixed blood. In recent years the status has become more socially acceptable, even a source of pride.

For the past two or three generations in Texas, the older—and for the most part destroyed—native cultures have been studied as well as they can be. Native Americans have entered all forms of modern employment, some giving up what remains of their heritage and others trying to incorporate that heritage, if not the totally lost ways of life. Many have succeeded in this transition.

A few things yet remain. Native American oral (and, lately, written) literatures are now seen as worthwhile creations. In some Indian literature, this story is told from the native viewpoint, not in the cadences of European scholarship. But both versions are true.

Lindsay and Sally Poncho's wedding, c. 1894, the first Christian wedding of Alabama-Coushattas

Tiguas in ceremonial dress at Ysleta del Sur, 1936

The Anglo-American Texans

Texas, in the short space of 15 years—1821 to 1836—became, and has remained, Anglo-American.

Certainly, this change came about because of military conquest, but only in part. The Texan victory at San Jacinto in April of 1836 was decisive not only for Texas but also for all of North America. Yet the battle was only a part of a settlement story.

In three centuries of rule, Spain had been able to place only some 4,000 settlers in the Texas province. And in 1821 Spain opened the land to immigration. More than 30,000 Anglo-Americans arrived by 1836, many legally. The cultural revolution was largely over before military operations had begun.

The "Anglos" were not, and are not, a uniform group. They were largely English and Scottish and Welsh with liberal additions of Irish, Dutch, Danish, and German. The "English" themselves were a highly mixed Nordic-Germanic-Celtic stock. And many United States census counts accepted as Anglo-American anyone who said they were Anglo—or Caucasian or white, in some decades. Most individuals who came to Texas with this widely varied background had been living in the United States just long enough for accurate lineage to have slipped from mind...and from importance. Many were from the southeastern part of the United States, and all could have been called "United Statesians."

Some traits were fairly common. These Anglos came to Texas with more accumulated frontiering experience than most; they were intensely individualistic and had first-hand knowledge of revolu-

Stephen F. Austin, the Father of Anglo Texas

"The Reading of the Texas Declaration of Independence" by Fanny and Charles Normann

tion and the peculiar experiment of self-government; and they regarded land as an exploitable, nearly consumable commodity.

Southern European traditions, at the time, held different and less competitive ideas.

Although some Anglo-American individuals are known to have been in Spanish Texas with permission—Peter Davenport was a Nacogdoches merchant by 1794—few arrived before 1821. In 1820 Jane Wilkinson Long followed her revolutionary husband, Dr. John Long, to Bolivar Point. Left there during an agonizing winter while her husband failed in his filibustering efforts, she gave birth to a third daughter, the first Anglo child known to have been born in Texas. Jane Long became a permanent Texas resident.

And many Anglos came to Texas with the idea that, Spanish or Mexican or whatever, Texas (and most of North America) was destined to be Anglo (and within the United States). They defined the destiny.

Anglo-Saxons, ever since their shift from north central Europe into Britain more than 1,400 years ago—creating new cultures and mixed races even then—have moved west as rulers and conquerors. The tiny battle of San Jacinto is thus the confirmation of an Anglo-American Republic of Texas and the end of southern European rule in most of North America.

Not that the revolutionary story is one-sided in terms of provocation. In 1824 the young Mexican government adopted a new constitution, which pleased many Anglo-American settlers in the Mexican state of Coahuila y Tejas because of its similarities to the laws of their homeland. When Santa Anna abolished this constitution in his rise to absolute power, he directly incited revolution—not only among Anglos.

Thus, many of the Anglos beginning the insurrection later known as the Texas Revolution, 1835–1836, first fought as Mexican citizens against a hated tyrant. But the illegal government they set up was unquestionably revolutionary. The first Anglo gover-

Jane Long, the Mother of Texas

Social gathering, c. 1890

Stephen F. Austin

Stephen F. Austin, often called "the father of Anglo-American Texas" is a symbol of both Anglo resourcefulness and Anglo stereotype.

Austin took over the job of bringing in the first coherent group of Anglo settlers to Mexican Texas after the death of his father, Moses. Remarks in Stephen's letters hint at his motive.

In Texas he seemed, at first, to be on the side of a peaceful solution to the settlers' troubles and most willing to be a citizen of Mexico in a Mexican state. After a number of events, including his imprisonment in Mexico on insurrectionist charges, he opted for revolution.

But even before coming to Texas, a couple of years before his father started the project, Stephen had an Anglo North America on his mind. Speaking at a July 4, 1818, Independence Day celebration in Potosi, Missouri, then part of the Louisiana Territory, the young man revealed some early thoughts on Spanish Texas. He was most direct. For closing remarks, he claimed the "same spirit that for a time blazed forth in France . . . the same spirit that unsheathed the sword of Washington . . . will also flash across the Gulph of Mexico . . . [to] rescue Spanish America from the dominion of tyranny." He may have had in mind the Mexican revolution, which was foundering at the time. But like many Anglos, he was probably thinking of something else.

Stephen F. Austin brought more to Texas than a hope for a new life or settlers—he brought an Anglo Independence Day.

---

nor, Henry Smith, spoke strongly for independence, as did Robert McAlpin Williamson, who was quickly known as "the Patrick Henry of the Texas Revolution." He was proud of the title.

Even Anglos who had ties with the Spanish and Mexican governments and peoples were swayed. Erastus Smith, married into a local family and with no argument against Mexico, changed sides. He had been stopped by Mexican soldiers and not allowed to rejoin his family in San Antonio. James Bowie had been in Texas since 1828 and, like Smith, had married locally. Yet, after the loss of his wife, Ursula Veramendi, to cholera, he changed sides.

But most Anglo-American Texans on the side of independence, called Texians (and for a short while, Texicans), were newcomers. The Texas Declaration of Independence of March 2, 1836, was signed by 59 men. Of these, 52 were Anglo, and only eight had been in Texas longer than six years.

In the wake of revolution and during the Mexican War that followed, many Mexican families departed or were driven south to what was left of Mexico. Even the architecture of the only significant Spanish town in Texas, San Antonio, changed to Anglo design. Little more than mission walls, dusty acequias, and the ghosts of the plazas remained.

Not until the Mexican Revolution, 80 years later, did significant immigration from Mexico again reshape the South and Central Texas population.

Thus, Anglo-American individuals, men and women alike, literally became the significant majority culture of the Republic and the State of Texas. This culture established English (in several dialects) as the language in use, the major economic patterns, many social customs, dominant forms of settlement and land use, and most laws and forms of political organization.

Many of the images of Texas—cotton, corn, cattle, and oil—were largely developed by, if not brought by, Anglos. Naturally, the Anglos learned from the range cattle operations of the Spanish; they absorbed Spanish language terms; they altered European law to fit the land; they used worldwide, and former, talents to exploit Texas's natural oil; and they did not raise cotton in Texas before the natives or the Spanish but did raise it on their own terms. In an economic sense, they improved on all.

Over the course of their story, Anglos became the stereotypical Texans in the world's eyes. Fortunately and unfortunately, stereotypes contain many falsehoods but also much truth.

Herd with cowboys and chuck wagon, Abilene, 1911

Cotton gin at Yancey, c. 1914

Oil boomtown Desdemona, known as Hogtown, c. 1920

The English Texans

English architect Alfred Giles (c. 1875), designer of many buildings around Texas and Mexico

A Walk across Texas

Perhaps the first English in Texas were David Ingram, Richard Twide, and Richard Browne, seamen who were put ashore on the Mexican coast in 1568 by Captain John Hawkins. Hawkins, in league with the future Sir Francis Drake, had lost a disastrous battle with the Spanish.

The survivors of the sunken ships, crowded onto Hawkins's surviving *Minion*, elected not to perish by starvation on a return to England, but to be set ashore. Walking south, they could at least find the comforts of a Spanish prison.

Once ashore, David Ingram and his companions decided to walk north. This they apparently did, turning east across Texas's coastal plain to enjoy an eventual Atlantic rescue by a French ship.

Ingram wrote a short account of the journey, which appeared in print in 1589, a generally accurate description of the Gulf coastal areas. "The Countrey is good and most delicate," Ingram says, "having great plaines, as large & as fayre in many places as may be seene, being as plaine as a board: And then great & huge woods of sundry kind of trees . . . plants & busshes, bark that biteth like Pepper . . . with the fruitfull Palme tree & a great plentie of other swete trees to this Ingram unknowen.

"And after that plaines againe, and in other places great closes of pasture, environed with most delicate trees, instead of hedges: they being as it were set by the hands of men . . . and great Rivers, by reason that the lowe grounds there be so rancke, that the grasse groweth faster then it can be eaten. . . ."

Texans of English origin seem to be the least colony-minded people in the state. One reason is that the English are simply part of the "Anglo" majority that has formed Texas since the mid-1830s. English settlers are often invisible.

Some of the early English were not so invisible to the Spanish. John Hamilton visited the mouth of the Trinity River as a horse buyer about 1774 and purchased any available stolen livestock...an activity not overly welcomed by the Spanish. Yet, in 1792, John Culbert, a silversmith, was allowed to live in San Antonio. His skills were valuable.

Even if native English were few, English products were not. Suppliers to the world, the English manufactured, for example, the famous third model "Brown Bess," or East India musket. In .75 calibre, it was a powerful if short-range weapon. This was the most common firearm of the Texas Revolution, used by both sides.

English individuals did involve themselves in various empresario and colonization schemes. All were grandiosely planned; all were ineffective. John Charles Beales's Rio Grande Colony attracted a few families before it disbanded in the 1836 revolution; and the Peters colony, chartered by the Republic of Texas in 1841, resulted in only light settlement over an area now constituting 26 North Texas counties. The Colony of Kent was perhaps the most interesting English effort. A commercial venture of the Universal Emigration and Colonization Company of London, this colony was imagined as a socialistic, profit-making community. The founding company convinced more than 30 families to leave Liverpool, England, for Central Texas. Kent was founded during the cold January of 1851. Backers of the venture claimed that Kent would become the "first city" of Texas, but the colonists were ill-informed about frontier hardships, were not farmers, and were not given sufficient backing for the first year. Soon, they had scattered for other areas where life would be easier.

No settlement areas became distinctly English. Individuals came, however, and settled all over the state. Some quickly became prominent.

But the most obvious English influence before the 20th century was investment and land ownership in the Texas Panhandle. In the decade after 1880, English ranchers and investors (most of the latter never saw Texas) put more than $25 million into 20 million acres of land.

The Capitol Freehold Land and Investment Company, incorporated in London, was the largest Panhandle investor. This company initially stocked and operated the three-million-acre XIT ranch, the land which had underwritten the construction costs of the present state capitol building.

Thus, the English, by drilling water wells, building fences, and bringing in stock, initiated plains ranching. Numerous settlers of all ethnic groups and origins came as workers, ranchers, and farmers to the plains. Most of these ventures did not, however, prove magnificently profitable, at least for the investors. English investment fever cooled by the turn of the century.

Many "native" Texans expected the English who came to Texas to be stereotypical characters. Some were. Heneage Finch, Seventh Earl of Aylesford, arrived in Big Spring in 1883 after leaving England to escape a disastrous divorce scandal. Setting himself up as a small rancher, he bought the local hotel in order that he or his guests would always have a room when needed; he bought a local butcher shop so he would always have meat cut to his liking; and he bought the saloon to ensure a ready supply of whisky, a half gallon a day.

William Anson, a more typical younger son, who could, under British law, inherit little or nothing, came to Tom Green County in 1902. He was able to purchase a working ranch and turn it into a quarter-horse operation by supplying mounts to the British army. Anson introduced polo to Texas, became a citizen, and served as a captain in World War I.

The largest number of English immigrants to enter Texas, more or less at the same time, came in mid-century at the end of World War II. They were the brides of U.S. soldiers returning to their home state.

The account seems to accurately reflect many things Ingram could have seen—natives, buffalo, birds and animals, palm wine and grapes, tornados and local religions, musical instruments and weapons of war...But his account—after an initial printing in Hakluyt's *The Principall Navigations, Voiages and Discoveries of the English nation, made by Sea or ouer Land to the most remote and farthest distant Quarters of the earth at any time within the compasse of these 1500 yeeres*—was discredited.

Among Ingram's sightings were also elephants, what appear to be javelinas "twice as big as an Horse," gold nuggets "some as big as a mans fist," and rubies "4 inches long and two inches broad." During his visit Ingram also claimed to have exorcised a devil, one Colluchio, who was fond of appearing "in the likenesse of a blacke Dogge." Twenty years later and like many an explorer, he obviously allowed imagination to lace his words with even greater wonders.

But the account gave many readers a first description of the area that would be Texas.

Heneage Finch, Seventh Earl of Aylesford, 1883

William Anson (far left) *and friends playing polo in Valera*

English-owned JA Ranch Headquarters, 1907

The Hungarian Texans

Helen Újházy Madarász (c. 1890), first Hungarian businesswoman in Texas, successfully dealt in real estate and, with her son Ladislaus, established the first nursery in the area on land that is now the San Antonio Zoo and Brackenridge Park.

Hungary in east-central Europe is a land of many peoples. Magyar, German, Slav, Romanian, Romany, and Slovak have mingled for a thousand years. The Hungarians, the Magyar, are themselves immigrants from farther east. This is a land of overlapping traditions and many languages—a troubled place.

Hungary, notably from 1848 to 1956, was a homeland its sons and daughters were forced to leave. The reasons were the usual: failed revolutionary efforts to break away from conquerors, international war, and overpopulation during peacetime.

Those who left, many for the Americas, unfailingly retained their language, customs, foods, and dress to a noticeable degree and their pride of origin absolutely. In new homelands, such as Texas, they continued a social change and adaptation that began in 10th century Europe.

The revolution of 1848–1849 directed against Austrian rule caused the exile of many soldiers and civil leaders, often the educated nobility from the highly stratified culture of Eastern Europe. People of the lower economic class had no means to leave; many of the rulers did.

László Újházi was a former civil governor of the Komárom fortress at the time of the 1848 revolution. Coming to San Antonio with others from the losing side, Újházi became the leader of what was perhaps Texas's first small Hungarian center. One of his daughters, Helen, became Texas's first Hungarian businesswoman.

Joe Petmecky came to New Braunfels in 1845, even before the outbreak of revolutionary feeling in Hungary, then set up a gunsmith shop in Austin. Petmecky became famous for his master craftsmanship and was soon known for his inventions. One idea that made him famous in the American West was the spring-shank steel spur. If a cowboy was thrown from his horse, the spur would open and fall away, rather than remain strapped on and possibly cause a broken ankle.

Dr. Arthur Wadgymár settled at Carrizo Springs in 1880; he was typical of the early Hungarian arrivals: professionals and craftspeople.

Hungarians in Texas were seriously split by the Civil War; some willingly enlisted, some were conscripted, and some became Union soldiers.

Between 1880 and 1920, like so much of Europe, Hungary provided agricultural immigrants. Under Austrian domination but in relative peace many of the years from 1849 to World War I, the country felt the pressure of overpopulation. So farming families came to Texas.

Following World War I, Hungary, on the losing side, was literally dismembered. Three-quarters of its land and population was put under other rulers. In World War II Hungary, joining Germany in an effort to regain territory, faced Russia—and lost.

In 1944 the Red Army advanced into Budapest, and many Hungarians left their homeland.

Under Communist rule few people were allowed to leave the shattered country. The subsequent Budapest uprising of 1956

J.C. Petmecky's gun shop, Austin, 1925— J.C. is seated; behind him is Howell Petmecky (at left) and Robert Felix.

resulted in another failure. Thousands fled west and, just as a century before, many of the refugees were well educated and technically trained.

Some individuals, such as Rose and Steve Safran, walked into Austria with little more than the clothes they wore and were eventually welcomed into the United States. The Safrans made San Antonio their home.

Today, a scattering of Hungarians, some native, most descended from earlier arrivals, live across Texas in urban areas. Individuals have entered the arts, investment and professional services, and politics.

Alois Goebel and his musical group, which played at the Menger Hotel, San Antonio, early 1900s—The three young women on the right are his daughters.

Ludwig Varga's saddlery store, Cuero—Several generations of the Varga family owned or worked in saddlery shops in San Antonio and Cuero. Their saddles were in great demand because of their high quality.

The Scottish Texans

Scots came to Texas as individuals and very small groups of families, not as colonists. Their notable activities and few settlement patterns showed them in the light of rigorous uniqueness rather than the clan-forming reputation known in Europe.

Some of the first Scots in Texas were explorers, mapmakers, and naturalists. William Dunbar and Thomas Drummond were both naturalists commissioned to report on the Texas area. Dunbar was chosen by U.S. President Thomas Jefferson in 1805 for explorations as political as scientific; Drummond reported to the University of Glasgow.

Later Scots came as families and developers. Neil McLennon, from the Isle of Skye, after stops in North Carolina and Florida, arrived on the coast of Texas with a group of friends and family in their own three-masted schooner. Moving inland, they suffered Indian attacks in Robertson's colony in 1838. McLennon continued on with his family to become an early settler on the Brazos near present Waco. McLennon County bears his name.

Many of the Clan Cameron found Texas exciting enough for a home. Among them was John Cameron, who came to Texas in 1827, bought land, and by 1835 was a secretary in the state government at Monclova. But he allied himself with the revolutionaries and joined the siege of Béxar.

Ewen Cameron arrived during the Texas Revolution, enlisted in the army, and later received land warrants which he claimed in San Patricio County. There he participated in frontier defense vigorously enough to earn the name "Bruce of the West."

Ewen Cameron's execution after the "Black Bean Episode" in 1843

Later, at the battle of Mier, when Texan forces were captured by Mexican troops, Cameron fought with rocks because he could not reload fast enough. As a prisoner in 1843, he was elected commander by the Texans when they were forced to draw black and white beans to determine who would be executed. Cameron drew a white bean, giving him the choice of life, a choice he could not take. He was shot after he attempted to escape.

Not all Scots were remembered as warriors. William Cameron, who did serve in the Civil War, was a lumberyard owner in Dallas and Denison. Later moving his operations to Waco, his William Cameron Company was eventually in charge of 60 retail locations. Before his death Cameron established himself in the timber and sawmill business, as a flour mill operator, and as a banker.

In the 1880s a number of Scottish stonecutters were contracted to make the journey to Texas as a group. Texas granite had been chosen for much of the new state capitol design, and native Scots brought experience with hard stone. Originally hired as strikebreakers themselves, the Scots faced other labor disputes while on the capitol job, but they cut and finished much of the stone for the present building. A few stayed in Texas and added their skills to later construction projects.

From 1890 to 1936, the Matador Land and Cattle Company, operating in the Panhandle and backed with Scottish money, was led by manager Murdo Mackenzie. The Matador herd, at 70,000 peak, was long regarded as one of the best in the United States.

Beginning just before the start of the 20th century, Texas Scots organized. By 1890 the Universal Order of Scottish Clans had a few lodges in Texas and was well established several decades later. The Scottish Society of Texas, dating from 1963 with a representation of more than 50 clans, holds annual Highland Games. "The Gathering of the Clans" is an often-held competition of field events, piping, and dancing in Salado.

These events, new only to Texas, provide Scottish identity for individuals who otherwise blend easily into Texas culture.

(Above) *Murdo Mackenzie, manager of the Matador Land and Cattle Co.;* (below) *the annual Gathering of the Scottish Clans of Texas, 1971*

Scottish stonecutters working on the Texas capitol in Austin, 1880s

The Irish Texans

Margaret Heffernan Borland was a child in the first group of McMullen-McGloin colonists in 1829. Thrice widowed, she became a rancher in Victoria County. In 1873 she led a drive of her own cattle up the trail to Kansas, but died of "trail fever" shortly after reaching her destination.

Harry McArdle

Irish Artists

Art—writing, painting, sculpture, music—has always been a part of Irish life. Harry Arthur McArdle of Belfast came to Texas after he had established himself as a producing artist, following a stint as a draftsman for the Confederate Navy and serving as topographical mapmaker for General Robert E. Lee. Settling at In-

The Irish have early connections with Texas and a long history filled with oppression, violence, individual ingenuity, faith, and exciting stories.

Long under English domination, the Irish have always left their homeland, in numbers large and small, to find fortune elsewhere. The *ad interim* governor of Texas in 1767 was Hugo Oconór, whose name leaves no doubt of origin. He was not the only Irish soldier or administrator or adventurer to enter the service of another country more congenial than England. Some were independent agents. Philip Nolan of Belfast was well known for efficient horse trading and illegal mapping in Spanish Texas. The latter occupation led to his death in 1801.

Father Juan Augustín Morfi, with a name as obvious as any Irish priest, came on a government inspection trip to the Texas area in 1777. His *History of Texas* is one of the earliest and best accounts of the land and people.

Nearly in the same tradition, Father Michael Muldoon, born in Ireland but in the service of Spain, left with Don Juan O'Donoju for the New World. O'Donoju became the last viceroy of Mexico. After Spain's expulsion Father Muldoon became priest to Austin's colony in 1831. In the colony under Mexican rule, everyone was Catholic—officially.

Some colonists saw Muldoon as a friend, others not. He was a friend of Santa Anna at times, visited Stephen F. Austin in his Mexico prison, and stayed in Texas after the revolution. In 1839 he called himself "Vicar General of the Catholic Communities of the Free and Independent Republic of Texas."

Irish families settled in small groups in many areas of Texas but made up the greatest percentage of the San Patricio and Refugio colonial populations before the Texas Revolution. Here, McMullen and McGloin as well as Power and Hewetson in 1828 were allowed to set up colonial areas north and west of modern Corpus Christi and bring in Irish families. Rumor, and some fact, attest that the Catholic Irish were seen by the Mexican government as good, loyal buffer colonies between themselves and the troublesome Anglos. Even so, many Irish were members of Stephen F. Austin's colony to the east, and after the start of the revolution, the Mexican army became well aware on which side the Irish stood. The Irish colonists near present Corpus Christi lived in one of the lines of march for the Mexican army. So, in today's terms, the Irish became excellent guerrilla soldiers.

Even their music was revolutionary. At San Jacinto two fifers and a drummer played "Will You Come to the Bower." The music is a British army tune, and the words are an Irish love song by Sir Thomas Moore, whose *Irish Melodies* were popular in Europe, particularly among Irish nationalists. The lyrics, by today's standards and unlike many Irish love lyrics, are only mildly suggestive. Some verses later were printed in Texas schoolbooks.

Texas Irish, during the revolution, did not spend all their time singing. Some 25 Irishmen signed the early Goliad Declaration of Independence, 11 died at the Alamo, 14 were with Fannin at Goliad, and about 100 fought at San Jacinto—a seventh of Sam Houston's army. Texas became a defended home.

In the next 50 years, Ireland was wracked by economic oppression and famine. The old country sent many settlers to Texas.

Some of the newcomers' work was stereotypical. The later 19th century Irish, arriving in substantial numbers after other established groups—as well as being Catholic, strange talkers, and considered "dumb" in the prejudice of the day—received the worst jobs: day labor. In Texas Irish crews worked east to west on the Southern Pacific railway. This route, the second transcontinental link in the U.S., was finished near Langtry. Even the railroad handcar, the velocipede car, became the "Irish Mail."

The Irish, in fact, entered most lines of work. John William Mallet, a Dubliner and professor of analytical chemistry, supported the South as a Confederate cavalryman after working as a chemist for the Geological Survey of Alabama in 1855. He became a professor of chemistry and physics and faculty chairman for the first session of the new University of Texas, never renouncing his European citizenship.

Today, more than a half million Texans identify themselves as Irish—direct descendants or recent arrivals. A number of Irish fraternal and social organizations exist in Texas, including the Irish Cultural Society of San Antonio; the Harp and Shamrock Society of Texas, a division of the Ancient Order of Hibernians; and a chapter of the Friendly Sons and Daughters of St. Patrick.

dependence, Texas, with his wife, Jennie Smith of Virginia, he taught art and developed an interest in Texas history. He soon secured commissions to paint notable Texans and Texas events. Well known are his portraits of Sam Houston and Jefferson Davis. His battle scenes, such as *Dawn at the Alamo* and *The Battle of San Jacinto*, both of monumental size, hang in the state capitol in Austin. They are not historically accurate but have created heroic myth.

Of Irish descent but born in Illinois, Charles Franklin Reaugh (the name Castlereaugh was shortened by the family), became Texan through a parental move to Kaufman County. Reaugh (pronounced "Ray" in Texas) sketched cattle, particularly longhorns, as a child, then began art training in St. Louis. He studied in Paris and Holland.

Returning to Texas, Reaugh set up a studio at his parents' house in Dallas, spent as much time as he could in field sketching, and taught. His students were expected to camp out with him, in rain or heat, with the rattlesnakes in West Texas.

Favoring pastels because they could be used with some ease in the field, he captured the cattle, sunsets, plains, and mountains of the state. Also an inventor and photographer, Reaugh patented a rotary industrial pump design and supported the Dallas Art Association. But most of his talent was invested in art. He invented new pastels, drawing paper and boards, a portable easel, and supply boxes—necessities for the artist who works outside a studio.

Reaugh remained devoted to field painting. "It is the beauty of the great Southwest as God has made it that I love to paint," he said. His most common advice was simple: "No man can serve two masters, and do justice to either."

He copyrighted a classification chart for North American animals and is called "Dean of Texas Artists"—and "Longhorn Leonardo."

Margaret Mary Healy Murphy, c. 1870, who founded the first religious order in Texas to educate black children— Today the Sisters of the Holy Spirit work out of about 40 missions in three states, and their multifaceted program is nondenominational and multiethnic. The original school opened by Mother Margaret Mary in San Antonio is now the Healy-Murphy Center for educating school dropouts.

The Shamrock Hose Company, fire-fighting unit for "Irishtown" in Corpus Christi

The Danish Texans

Danish Texans, perhaps, are the best model of a small group going through the acculturation process—that is, becoming Texans and adding to the concept of what it is to be Texan.

Never numbering more than one in 3,000 Texans, persons of immediate Danish heritage are nevertheless notable in the last 170 years. Danish immigrants came for varied motives, but for most the reasons were land and economic prosperity. They are often known for their individuality...in some cases, eccentricity.

A young Danish painter, Charles Zanco, left no record of his motive for coming to Texas in the summer of 1835. He designed one of several early Texas flags: the blue, single-star "Independence" flag of the revolutionary Lynchburg company. This flag, "Captain Scott's Flag," was carried at the battle of Concepción and the siege of Béxar. Zanco died at the Alamo.

Christian Dorbrandt served in the Mexican War, then was transferred by the U.S. Army as quartermaster sergeant to Ft. Croghan near Burnet. He retired about 1855 but stayed in Texas. His marriage to Annie Dunlavy of Ireland and their 14 subsequent children did not remove the warfare in his blood: they perhaps contributed. While Dorbrandt served in the Civil War, Annie kept armed guard at home against Indian threat. Dorbrandt delighted in serving as a Texas Ranger until he was past 60.

Christian Mathisen and his wife, Emily Striegler, of Fredericksburg became known for their storytelling. Emily told fairy tales in the manner of Hans Christian Andersen, and Christian recounted stories of the Norse pagan gods in resounding verse.

Informal groups of Danish families settled in northern Lee County, known as "Little Denmark," as well as in Williamson County and in Rocky Hill near Fredericksburg, but the rural Wharton County colony of Danevang, the Danish Field, is the only coherent Danish colony in the state.

In the late summer of 1894, the first settlers of Danevang, mostly Danes who had spent some years on the United States' northern plains, arrived in Texas, finding land south of El Campo.

The Carl Jensen family home near Danevang

The P.J.A. Petersen family on their farm near Danevang, c. 1906

H.P.N. Gammel

In the face of adverse weather, Gulf hurricanes, and the necessity of raising unfamiliar crops, the colony did not initially prosper. The Danes came with the idea of showing off their north-country farming skills and preserving a distinctly Danish way of life. They did neither. But they stayed, eventually a hundred families strong.

Two questions were posed, in Danish verse, by P.J. Agerskov-Petersen for the 50th anniversary of Danevang in 1944:

Er der ikke Spor tilbage	Is there nothing left whatever
fra de gode, gamle Dage?	from the good, old days?
Er der mon et lille Minde,	Is there, I wonder, a small reminder
om en enkelt Mand og Kvinde?	of any single man or woman?

The questions can be raised not only of Danevang but of all settlement in Texas. And the answer is yes, there are many accomplishments—and many memories.

Ansgar Lutheran Church in Danevang, 1908

Hans Peter Nielsen Gammel

Hans Peter Nielsen Gammel became one of the most well-known Danish Texans.

Hans married Anna Marie Andersen in Denmark when he was 16. Facing a lack of opportunity after 1874, he followed his sister to the United States "to dig some gold and send for the family."

Gammel found no literal gold mine, but he and his brother Niels saw much of the central and western United States. Gammel mentioned later, "What we did and how is a dead letter. I never killed anybody and never robbed anybody and I hardly ever carried a gun." And he did send for the family; they eventually caught up with him in Austin.

Over the next few years, Gammel set up a retail shop selling stationery, jewelry, lemonade, and books. The books took over. In the words of the locals, Gammel's store changed from a "lemonade stand with books and trinkets for sale" to a "bookstand where lemonade was sold."

When the state capitol building burned in 1881, Gammel contracted the salvage job and rescued thousands of pages of charred, water-soaked state records. He entered the publishing business, became state printer, and produced, among many titles, the *Laws of Texas, 1822-1897*. This 10-volume set, preserving the records saved from the destroyed capitol, was an instant classic and remains the fundamental collection of Texas law.

Gammel's letterheads became legendary, graced with such headings as: "The Oldest Book Store in the State, Established in 1877. The Proprietor, Gammel, was born in Denmark, rich and good looking—not so now" and "Capital Stocks $000,000.00." In fact, Gammel did a good business and became internationally famous.

His desk, topped by an antique pistol, was home to a trained mouse. Close by lounged his dog, Bill, who had a charge account at the nearby market and drugstore. And Gammel's infamous Copenhagen Punch, served at home, remained a secret composition which could stop anyone in his tracks.

But Gammel's "jollities" did not obscure his reputation as The Texas Bookman. His store invoices bore the line "If it's a book... Get it at Gammel's." One could. Many of his rare books are now in the library of the University of Texas at Austin.

The Norwegian Texans

J.R. Reiersen, the Father of Norwegian Immigration

Elise Wærenskjold (c. 1857), a woman far beyond her times: schoolteacher; champion of social causes; briefly editor of Reiersen's monthly magazine in Norway; then, in Texas, noted writer for Norwegian papers on the benefits of immigration to America and the beauties of Norwegian life in Texas

Texas Norwegians, arriving and settling as small rural groups, have been few. The 1900 census listed a peak number of 1,356 native Norwegians in the state, a total that declined to 1,000 in 50 years. Today, some 95,000 Texans claim Norwegian descent.

Most of the emigration came from rural areas in Norway to rural areas in Texas. The first known individual was Johannes Nordboe, who, in 1841 when he was over 70, settled near Dallas with his family.

Johan Reinert Reiersen attempted a colony in Henderson County in 1845; another group influenced by the earlier arrivals moved to Van Zandt and Kaufman Counties between 1846 and 1853. Reiersen, a journalist, editor, and author, had been sponsored in 1843 by a group of prospective emigrants and financiers to tour the United States and report settlement possibilities.

This Reiersen did—he heard about Texas in New Orleans. Visiting the republic, he was given a welcome by Sam Houston. Reiersen apparently was convinced; returning to Norway, he so complimented Texas and so insulted the opportunities in Norway that many Norwegians were outraged.

Deciding to emigrate, Reiersen left for Texas, arriving in 1845. He established the magazine *Norge og Amerika* before leaving, turned it into an emigration newsletter, and edited it from Texas.

After annexation he brought settlers to Henderson County in the new state, where he was joined also by his two brothers. They named the place Normandy, but after 1848 the name yielded to Brownsboro. Later, an additional area at Four Mile Prairie on the border of Kaufman and Van Zandt Counties was established as a colonial area with a small number of families. Reiersen died in Texas, still writing, always irritating native Norwegians by telling them Texas was better than their homeland.

Cleng Peerson, Ole Canuteson, and Carl Quæstad walked the Bosque River and led a few Norwegians into the new Bosque County in 1854. West of Waco, the community of Norse was for a time the largest concentration of Norwegians in Texas. The area remains home to about a hundred people today; many are descendants of the Norwegian arrivals. The church community has maintained one custom into recent years, an annual *smörgåsbord* held at Our Savior's Lutheran Church.

Cleng Peerson, responsible for much of the Norwegian immigration to the eastern United States as well as to Texas, is buried at the Norse church.

Norwegian immigration lasted somewhat past the Civil War, and individual families did maintain some Old World customs. But, separate as most homesteads were, Norwegian as a language disappeared in all practical use by 1940.

The Norwegian Society of Texas, with groups in several Texas cities, was founded in 1975 to preserve, and certainly to replicate, Norse heritage. Members of this group still emphasize their Viking heritage and costume—which were never actually a part of Texas culture until the last two decades.

The first post office in Norse was also a store. Ole Ringness (at left) was a substitute carrier.

Ole Ringness

Ole Ringness, born in Norway, came to Texas with his parents in 1852, stopping in Reiersen's Prairieville settlement. Typhoid fever and drought caused a move to Bosque County, west of Clifton, where Ringness became a mail carrier between that area and Ft. Worth.

Ringness noted, one long and particularly muddy day, that wagon wheels, cupped on the axle, threw out a good deal of dirt to the side. Being a farmer, Ringness immediately had the idea of a new plow blade, shaped like a saucer or a disk. This plow, he knew, would work well in wet black soil. He soon made several models in his father's blacksmith shop.

In 1872 Ringness went to New York City to register a patent. He carried a considerable amount of money, intending to visit Norway after the conclusion of his business.

From New York the family was notified of his death. The cause of death was not, and is not, known; his place of burial could never be determined. And, according to a patent office, the plow design had not been registered, but a patent could be issued for a $5 fee. The family did not pursue the patent registration.

Sometime later disk plows were on the commercial market, patented by J.I. Case Plow Company, as a successful, popular improvement for many soil conditions.

The Norway Mill in Norse, built in the 1880s

Immigrant attitudes toward Norway were often like Johan Reiersen's, full of honest respect but critical of a country that could not provide for the working class. An old emigrant song is very direct:

Farewell, thou Mother Norway,
  now I must leave thee.
Because thou fostered me,
  I give thee many thanks.
All too sparing wert thou in
  providing food for the
  throng of thy laborers.
Thou, who gavest more than
  enough to thy well-
  schooled sons.

The Swedish Texans

Fred and Olga Nygren Bergman with Ruth

The Bergman Letters

Few narrative accounts exist today about or by the Swedish Texans. Of wonderful exception are the letters from the Bergman brothers.

Carl Johan Bergman and his brother, Clæs Fredrik (called "Fred"), came to Texas, choosing the New Sweden area east of Austin in 1883. They soon operated a farm in the community of Lund and wrote many letters over the decades to their sisters in Sweden.

The letters give a remarkably detailed account of how Texas was seen by immigrants. Often signing the letters together, they compliment and criticize Texas. One thing new was the ever-shifting Texas weather, as Carl writes:

"I wish that I could describe Texas for you, but it would be too difficult, for much is still strange to me.... When it begins to rain, it can last for long periods of time and the same is true for periods of no precipitation....

"The soil here is of such a consistency, that when it rains, we can neither ride nor walk, it becomes so muddy, so then we have to stay inside long hours. Or, if we do go out, we have to ride horses. Winter is variable, sometimes warm, sometimes cold. We have no winter before Christmas.... Fred and I have slept outside on the porch for over a week . . . it is so warm in our room that we can't sleep there.

"I don't think you'd recognize us; we have become brown and lean...."

But Fred, writing years later in 1908, had become used to the climate, claiming, "I would freeze to death in an instant if I were at home." And, married by then to Olga Nygren, he noted his lack of attraction to Texas women. "Here in Texas, women are in general small and thin, the climate is the reason."

Fred summed up the Swedish Texan experience: "... Texas is a place for the poor to work their way up by means of work and thrift. Poor Swedes come here practically all the time, and in a few years they are independent. This place is not for a lazy bones but for the diligent."

Most immigrants coming from Sweden to Texas arrived in a 60-year period, from 1848 to about 1910.

The first group of Swedes was recruited by Swen Magnus Swenson, who had come to Texas in 1838 and profited from a plantation in Ft. Bend County. Friend to Sam Houston, Swenson was convinced to help bring Swedish families to Texas. An initial group of 25 came in 1848.

Soon, Swenson's uncle, Swante Palm, had arrived, and the two became successful business partners. They operated an informal immigration company which paid travel expenses on credit or in return for indentured labor.

Other individuals and families, both in Sweden and the north-central United States, heard about Texas possibilities and came. By the turn of the century, more than 4,000 Swedes were in the state.

Swedish settlement was rural at first but near urban centers. Later settlement patterns were urban. Svenska kullen, or "Swedish hill," in downtown Austin was home to almost 50 Swedish families. Settlers located in and near Austin, Dallas, Ft. Worth, and Waco, as well as smaller towns. Some Texas place names indicate a Swedish origin or namesake, even though all did not become places of exclusive Swedish settlement: Lund, New Sweden, Swedonia, West Sweden, Palm Valley, Swensondale, Stockholm, Ericksdahl (Ericsdale), and Govalle (dialect for "good grazing").

From 1896 to 1982, the *Texas-Posten* was the newspaper for Swedes in Texas. Two others, the *Södra Vecko-Posten* (1882) and the *Texas-Bladet* (1900–1909) had short but influential lives.

Swedish interests established Trinity Lutheran College in Round Rock and Texas Wesleyan College in Austin, but both ceased operations because of a lack of financial backing.

Today, some 160,000 individuals in Texas claim Swedish descent. In some locations, families still prepare "traditional" foods, and some individuals take pride in learning Swedish. In fact, Texas Swedish as a spoken (or read) language has been remarkably durable. Even though Swedish Lutheran and Methodist churches abandoned the language over a generation ago, the *Texas-Posten* published a quarter of its copy in Swedish until its end. In the 1980s the *SVEA Nytt*, a newsletter, was published by an organization of Swedish-speaking women.

For the most part, however, descendants today are almost completely assimilated into the host culture.

A number of cultural events were held in 1988 on the 150th anniversary of the first arrivals, including an official visit by King Carl XVI Gustaf and Queen Silvia of Sweden.

Quotations from Swante Palm

"The chief characteristic of weather in Texas is not variety, but surprise."

"The human being is the only animal with the gift of self-deception."

Swen Magnus Swenson

Swante Palm in his library, c. 1894

Swenson and Palm

Two men were directly responsible for the bulk of Swedish immigration to Texas: Swen Magnus Swenson and Swante Palm.

Swenson was the first to arrive in Texas, in 1838. Working his way up from peddler of mercantile goods to plantation owner, he was joined in 1844 by his uncle Swante Palm, a newspaper editor, court clerk, and secretary. The two men were overwhelmingly successful business partners as well as independent operators.

Swenson, establishing a mercantile business in Austin with Palm, became a land dealer. Buying land certificates and investing in the Buffalo Bayou, Brazos and Colorado Railway, he became one of the top landowners in the state. Swenson established the SMS Ranch and maintained a fleet of freight wagons to sell goods in West Texas. In Swenson's words, his wagons carried "boots and shoes, Hats, Hardware, Holloware, Earthenware, Woodware, Blacksmith's tools, Iron, Steel and Nails; a General Assortment of Groceries, Flour, Tobacco, Rice, etc.; whiskey, brandies, Holland gin, Rum, Sherry, Madeira, Port and Claret wine by the box or the barrel, oils, Paints, Window-Glass and Putty, Bagging and Bale Rope, Powder Shot and Lead; cooking stoves and office stoves, ploughs, hoes...." Anything anyone would need...

Swenson remained neutral as the Civil War approached, an unusual accomplishment due to his ability to export cotton as an agent for the Swedish government, his investments, and friendship with Governors Sam Houston and Francis Lubbock. Even so, he joined Houston in an effort to counter Texas secession. Houston, whose ideas were rarely low-profile, planned an independent Texas army. Swenson, to be made a colonel for his efforts, was to provide troop supplies. Although plans failed, the activity was hardly considered neutral. By 1863 Swenson had left Texas in fear of his life. He lived thereafter in Monterrey, Mexico, Sweden, and New York without dissolving his Texas ties or investments. He regularly visited the state.

Swante Palm, in addition to joining his nephew in various business ventures, became a La Grange postmaster and diplomatic secretary to Thomas William Ward, United States consul in Panama.

Writing in favor of slavery, but not participating, Palm maintained a careful neutrality during the Civil War and was in an excellent political position during Reconstruction. He became a Travis County justice of the peace and a member of the Austin City Council. He was also an amateur scientist who turned professional. He served as meteorologist for the first Texas Geological and Agricultural Survey.

Appointed vice consul for Norway and Sweden in 1866, Palm worked continuously for Swedish immigration to Texas.

Palm built a private library during his life totaling over 12,000 volumes. Many he had read carefully, as shown by his marginalia in English, French, Swedish, Norwegian, German, and Latin. He donated his library to the University of Texas in 1897, a gift which increased university library holdings by 60 percent. As late as 1970, some of his volumes remained in use on the regular shelves of the library. His books are now in special collections.

New Sweden Lutheran Church, 1920s

The African-American Texans

Many Africans who arrived in Texas before 1860 were brought in as slaves; others came as free people, indentured servants, or escaped slaves. Whatever the case, their story is linked directly to Spanish and Anglo-American settlement which largely defined Texas.

Slavery—the ownership of human beings by others to perform labor—is as old as civilized humanity from Rome to China and has been carried on as a systematic process by all major cultures for economic, though brutal, reasons. Until the modern era, humans were the most efficient source of intelligent power. Except for the brute force of oxen and elephants, camels and horses, llamas and dogs, humans provided the energy to plant and build for masters who could force the labor.

Most of the first Africans in the New World were brought by European entrepreneurs. Although the Spanish did enslave Indians in the service of agriculture, mining, and personal needs, as the natives died of overwork or disease or chose to move on, the Europeans began kidnapping Africans to fill their places. Significant numbers of Africans were soon to be found in all reaches of the Spanish empire, but few in the frontier province of Texas. Many of these were of mixed heritage, and some individuals bought or were granted freedom. Spanish law, unlike later United States law, allowed freed people all legal rights except government office employment.

At the time of the Mexican Revolution of 1821, the new government technically made slavery illegal. Anglo-Americans who chose this decade to enter Texas from the east brought in "indentured servants" around the edges of Mexican law. After the Anglo-American revolution of 1836, Texas became slave-holding territory for the next quarter century.

And in all these years, whether legally possible or not, some blacks became free, and a few came as freedmen...a very few.

Also, in all of these years, individuals of African heritage distinguished themselves as soldiers, explorers, educators, builders, and settlers.

Most African-American residents of Texas today—nearly 12 percent of the total population—originated from blacks brought by Anglos before 1860 largely to East Texas, then an agricultural extension of the United States' South, or they came for economic reasons in contemporary times.

The distribution of blacks in Texas reflects this story: most live in the southeast quadrant of the state, many of these still rural, and in all metropolitan areas.

The story of African-American settlement is also reflected in the names given to, or taken by, the people. Earlier Africans, taken as slaves from dark-skinned cultures, were called blacks—Negroes. By no means "uncultured," these became the stereotype blacks to Europeans: *los negros esclavos*.

Europeans used the Spanish word, or "Moor," or the names of areas of Africa from which slaves were taken. Thus, "Negro" became a hated word for later generations. "Afro-American" and

Tillie Brackenridge on the porch of Mrs. William Vance's residence at Navarro and Travis Streets in San Antonio, where she was employed, c. 1900— Tillie formerly was a slave in James Vance's elegant home on East Nueva Street and told of seeing Robert E. Lee, a frequent visitor to the house.

"African American" are modern terms, indicating a great truth: many African traditions—at least in detail—were stripped from the people in a deliberate way. A forcible relocation into another culture, a larger and more powerful culture, results in much loss. This, of course, is true for all groups entering Texas or any "host" culture in relatively small numbers, whether by force or not.

Yet all groups retain something of their heritage, and so did Africans. But succeeding generations were, for better or worse, greatly changed...into Americans.

The term "black," a simple translation, is widely accepted, particularly by the younger generation, as a proper political and cultural term.

Thus, African Americans in Texas, neither a single people nor a group with definite borders, have an immensely interesting history and possess a story that has been a large part of Texas.

Even considering the overwhelming fact of slavery and its resulting anonymity, many African-American Texans are known for individual contributions.

The first known by name was a personal slave of Andrés Dorantes, a Moor called Estevan, who was one of four to survive the Narváez expedition's disaster in 1528. Estevan, Dorantes, Alonso del Castillo, and Alvar Núñez Cabeza de Vaca survived years in what is today Texas and finally returned to Mexico to tell their stories. One of these stories—that north of Mexico were cities of gold—fired further Spanish exploration. And one of the later efforts was led by the durable Estevan.

The villa of San Antonio de Béxar—under several names and often with nearly the rank of provincial capital—was always home to blacks who engaged in jobs from agriculture to blacksmithing, teaching to selling merchandise. The Spanish, unlike later Anglos, accepted the facts of intermarriage and individual accomplishment without denying the necessity of slavery.

After 1836 the technicality of freedom was denied to blacks in the republic and later the state, but a few free individuals nevertheless called Texas home.

Samuel McCulloch Jr. was one of the first men to be wounded in the Texas Revolution, at Goliad in 1835. Scout Hendrick Arnold led a column of Texan volunteers in the later, successful attack on San Antonio. Samuel G. Hardin fought at San Jacinto. Such individuals, few in number, were either given special legisla-

Samuel McCullough Jr. charging the fort at Goliad, October 1835, from "The Battle of Goliad" by Kermit Oliver

"A" Troop, 10th Cavalry, U.S. Army, c. 1890— "Buffalo Soldiers"

Dr. J. Mason Brewer

John Mason Brewer is known as a scholar, teacher, historian, folklorist, and storyteller who was perhaps the first Texan to tell the full range of African-American experience from formal historical accounts to the excitement and accuracy of folktales. He spoke of the entire range of black Texas experience.

Brewer was born in Goliad in 1896, the son of a cowboy. Schooled in Austin, he advanced through Wiley College to a master's degree from Indiana and Ph.D. from Paul Quinn College. Combining academic credentials and a very active personal life, Brewer was qualified to observe and speak—as few before or after—on a broad range of experience.

For more than a quarter century, he worked and taught at East Texas State University. He was a longtime member of the Texas Folklore Society and served as council member and vice president for the American Folklore Society.

His accomplishments range from an academic study of Reconstruction times in Texas—*The Negro Legislators of Texas*—to the collections of African-American folktales and life such as *Dog Ghosts*. His *Aunt Dicey Tales* and *The Word on the Brazos* are still popular.

Brewer was also the first author and speaker to use black American dialect extensively in front of and to all audiences, particularly when dealing with folklore. Occasionally, he drew mixed reactions, from blacks and whites alike, because of the prejudicial feeling against the dialects commonly spoken by Texas blacks.

Brewer succeeded in defending black American vernacular as a literary dialect, but, above all, he presented the lives of African-American Texans truthfully with neither heroic overstatement nor apology. And he did this with much beauty.

tive permission to remain in Texas or benefited from local law looking the other way.

Others were never freed in any real sense. Chloe Stevens, born in 1794 and brought to Liberty County in the 1820s, was near the battle of San Jacinto and helped care for the wounded of both sides. She died in San Antonio in 1901 at the age of 107, after living several lifetimes as personal servant, slave, wife, and mother. She saw much of Texas history.

Most individuals were given the hard task of crossing from slavery before the Civil War to technical freedom thereafter.

Many blacks found military service a logical career. In Texas, and in much of the post-Civil War West, the Buffalo Soldiers became a frontier tradition. Black soldiers of the 9th and 10th Cavalries and the 24th and 25th Infantries protected settlement areas against Indian and renegade attack until near the turn of the century. The origin of the name "Buffalo Soldiers" is not known for certain. Some soldiers, in the cold of high plains winters, wore buffalo-hide robes and ponchos; some blacks had curly hair; and the soldiers had the determination and speed of the native animal. Certainly the name was given by the Plains Indians, perhaps for all these reasons.

And a single man could become a cowboy. Many did, and a few, such as Daniel Webster "80 John" Wallace, eventually owned their own ranches and herds. Wallace died a millionaire in 1939.

Also, after the Civil War, black families proved durable enough to weather the restrictive civil laws that replaced literal slavery for the next three generations. The tradition of sharecropping provided a bridge for some African Americans to a future not imagined by earlier generations, black *or* white, while others had brought with them skills such as metalworking and pottery making or had learned a trade under slavery and could practice it with profit. After June 19, 1865, Emancipation Day in Texas and a day still celebrated, men could set themselves up as weavers, potters, blacksmiths, masons, and carpenters. Today, no field of modern human endeavor lacks the names of African Americans.

John Dunn, Carson Wallace, Daniel Webster Wallace, and Charlie Hale preparing to ship cattle at the Silver Creek Ranch, Mitchell County

Black cowboys on the Rio Grande Plain, c. 1900

Opera singer and actor Jules Bledsoe, when he was appearing in Showboat *at the National Theater in Washington, D.C., February 1930—Born in Waco, Bledsoe studied music in Chicago, Paris, and Rome. After his first Broadway hit,* Showboat, *he sang in Europe and became well known. In his career he performed in operas, musicals, and motion pictures; he was also a pianist and composer. Bledsoe was just 45 years old and at the peak of his career when he died unexpectedly in Hollywood in 1943.*

The Jewish Texans

Judaism is a religion and also a way of life pervasive enough to create an identity as powerful as any other national, cultural, or ethnic group in the state. Judaism's earlier connection to a particular geography—and then for centuries to a lack of homeland—helped establish and maintain a worldwide cultural group.

The first Jews coming to Texas were notable individuals—and few. But by the mid-19th century, Jewish immigration followed typical patterns along trade and transportation routes and, generally, remained urban and involved families.

Spanish Texas did not welcome easily identifiable Jews, but they came in any case. Jao de la Porta was with Jean Lafitte at Galveston in 1816, and Maurice Henry was in Velasco in the late 1820s. Jews fought in the armies of the Texas Revolution of 1836, some with Fannin at Goliad, others at San Jacinto.

Adolphus Sterne, born in Germany, moved to Nacogdoches in 1826, already a friend of Sam Houston. Although he came to America to avoid military service, he sided with the Fredonian Revolution of 1826 and was soon smuggling guns in dry goods crates and gunpowder in coffee containers. In spite of this activity, Sterne served in public office under the Mexican government and later in both houses of the Texas state legislature.

Dr. Albert Levy became a surgeon to revolutionary Texan forces in 1835, participated in the capture of Béxar, and joined the Texas Navy the next year. Shortly after the Texas Revolution, in 1839, Rosanna Osterman became well known as a leader in Galveston's Jewish community. She remained in the city during the Federal capture of the port during the Civil War, acted as nurse to the wounded of both sides, then turned Confederate spy, carrying intelligence about the Federal occupation which helped Southern forces retake the city. At her death she bequeathed a fortune to various charities throughout the United States.

Certainly the first Jewish individuals came out of a sense of adventure, or fled hardships and oppression, or moved with a loved one, and the earliest did not always practice their faith openly. Later arrivals came as settlers seeking a new life in a congenial homeland.

Jews have, at times, been targets of oppression from Western Europe to Russia. In Texas, in most years, they found comparative freedom to practice their religion, follow their way of life, and seek opportunity for economic advancement.

Here Jews established a mercantile pattern in which individuals would arrive at a port or urban center and journey along well-established roads selling what they could. Finding a satisfactory business location, they would settle and, preserving their links to sources of supply, would provide a nucleus for others—a chain pattern.

Sanger, Marcus, Zale, Levy, and Sakowitz are only a few of the very well-known names that have defined the entrepreneurial spirit. And individuals have distinguished themselves in art, banking, ranching, law, medicine, and government.

Rabbi Henry Cohen (here at age 79) achieved a national reputation for philanthropic and humanitarian endeavor in his 62 years in Texas.

Front of Temple B'nai Israel in Galveston, which Henry Cohen was invited to lead in 1888

In the largest numbers, Texas's Jewish population lives in cities and always has. An urban Jewish community would develop from a collection of families. A Jewish cemetery usually was established, then benevolent societies, then a synagogue with a community center.

Some individuals arrived with considerable resources, some with only the clothes on their backs; most of them became productive citizens.

Known for their defense of individual social justice, Texas Jews have involved themselves in the changes of modern life while maintaining some of the oldest cultural customs in the world.

Joshua Furman reading the Torah at his bar mitzvah, San Antonio, May 1994

Wedding of Bessie Antweil and Labe H. Golden in Ft. Worth, December 1924

Sukkot meal in a sukkah at a Laredo Sunday School, c. 1935—Sukkot is the fall harvest festival held in memory of the ancestors who dwelt in the wilderness after fleeing Egypt. Jewish families build sukkahs (temporary huts) with roofs of green branches. At least once a day for eight days, families and friends share meals in the sukkah.

The Swiss Texans

The Swiss are only a small cultural representation in Texas, but, as the ethnic-studies cliché goes, they made "a contribution far greater than their actual numbers."

Generally, the Swiss had little reason for leaving their homeland or coming to Texas. Most Swiss taking leave of Europe in the 19th century simply sought greater opportunity or were moved by a spirit of adventure. They were also quick to assimilate into the culture of a new home, wherever they went.

They heard about possibilities in the Americas through the usual channels: newspapers, letters from wanderers, commercial advertising, and emigrant organizations.

A few schemes existed for mass emigration—one in 1819 with the goal of moving 10,000 Swiss to Texas was approved by the Spanish government—but all were failures.

The Swiss came as individuals and families, and they entered an astonishingly diverse number of occupations.

Henry and Louis Rueg were in Nacogdoches by 1823 as horse traders; Jean Louis Berlandier came as a professional botanist in 1828 at the invitation of the Mexican government and stayed to complete the first ethnographic description of Texas Indians; and Peter Fullinwider and his wife entered Mexican Texas, illegally, as the first Presbyterian missionaries.

Charles and Mary Amsler settled in Cat Spring, German country, in 1834, and both participated in the revolution two years later. They, and various family members, operated a farm, started a cotton gin, managed a stagecoach stop, and opened a lumber business. Andrew Baldinger was a Galveston banker. John Hermann, a veteran of Waterloo on the losing side, came to Houston with a wife, three children, and five dollars. Helped by the sale of his wife's jewelry, Hermann prospered as a baker. His son, George, bought land on which oil was fortuitously found and became a Houston philanthropist.

George Hermann—From modest beginnings, he achieved great wealth and gave his city of Houston a hospital; Hermann Square next to City Hall; and Hermann Park, an important recreational facility.

Christian Moser established the first of three Swiss-owned dairies in Dallas in 1873. Here he drives his dairy wagon in the 1880s.

John Jacob Rahm, a Texas Ranger, advised the German Prince Carl of Solms-Braunfels to buy the land on which New Braunfels was established; Henry Rosenberg of Galveston was a mercantile-business owner and banker; and Johann U. Anderegg produced Swiss cheese in Texas's Hill Country. Getulius Kellersberger, chief engineer for Confederate forces in Texas, became project director of a rocket battalion stationed in San Antonio, an effort which ended in spectacular, explosive failure.

Gustave Duerler turned pecan shelling into a Texas industry; Edward Walter Eberle, born in Denton of Swiss parentage, became admiral of the U.S. Pacific Fleet and Chief of Naval Operations; Karl Hoblitzelle organized the Interstate Amusement Company and literally developed the commercial theater in contemporary Texas; and Peter Mansbendel was one of the most original and creative woodcarvers of the 20th century. Godfred Fleury, a mural and fresco painter, also constructed parade floats and founded an advertising company. He was still going strong when, at the age of 68, he entered the University of Texas at Austin as a freshman engineering student. Of maternal Swiss descent, Dwight David Eisenhower was born in Texas and, with much military service in the state, often referred to Texas as home.

Swiss-Texan history reads like a breathless roster of accomplishment. It is.

Peter Mansbendel, master carver of all types of objects in many kinds of wood—He produced portraits, carvings of flora and fauna, bas relief panels, furniture, and decorative motifs for mantels, stairways, and doors.

Detail from a Mansbendel mantel carved in 1932

The German Texans

The Marienkirche in Fredericksburg, begun in 1860

A Sunday house in Fredericksburg

Texans of German birth or descent have, since the mid-19th century, made up one of the largest ethnic groups in the state. By 1850 they numbered five percent of the total population—a conservative count. The 1990 census listed more than 17 percent of the population, nearly three million individuals, claiming German heritage.

Germans who chose Texas as a home were, in the migrations from 1830 to 1900, anything but a uniform group. Early emigration came from a land of provinces and duchies, not a unified Germany, and from many backgrounds.

Johann Friedrich Ernst, even if he left the Duchy of Oldenburg just a step ahead of charges of embezzlement, was a born immigrant if anyone ever was. Learning of Stephen F. Austin's Texas colony, he had purchased a tract of land by 1831 and the next year had written letters to his homeland describing Texas as a paradise. The province of Texas, then a part of Mexico, only lacked German industry and genius.

Many came. Most of the Germans attracted by Ernst's letters, and by later colonial ventures, were peasants but not poor. This majority was laced with artisans, academicians, and professionals. Some were political refugees; a few fled religious persecution—families and individuals believing simply that their full economic and social potentials could not be realized in Europe.

But colonists they were. Typically, small groups of families living closely in Europe came to Texas, where they settled, again, as small groups living together. Most arrivals set up as farmers, the first near Friedrich Ernst in such places as Industry, Cat Spring, and Rockhouse.

Subsequent publicity about Texas and the republic's independence drew the attention of minor noblemen in the German states to the idea of investing in Texas. These noblemen were interested in philanthropically helping the German rural class but also wanted to find a source of raw materials. They may have hoped to develop political influence in a new country, and most certainly counted on personal profit. Their efforts, financially disastrous for them, did bring in more than 7,000 immigrants.

Many of the German colonists settled to the north and west of the Austin County Germans. Thus, a "German Belt" was created, stretching from Texas's Coastal Plain to the Hill Country, including the larger towns of New Braunfels and Fredericksburg.

German immigrants, attracted to colonial settlement in appreciable numbers and relatively isolated from others—the necessities for cultural preservation—maintained certain customs and most of the language.

Some, of course, dreamed of a New Germany...which did not come to pass; the Germans were not of a single culture.

For a time, the Pedernales River valley was known as the home of dancing and drinking Germans, the Lutheran and Catholic farmers who liked recreation. The upper valley of the Guadalupe was home to a good number of intellectuals and political refugees. Many of these were "free thinkers" or even, to the horror of conservative neighbors, atheists. The Llano valley was peopled by German Methodists, among other stern types, who avoided drinking and fraternal gatherings.

Professors and farmers came, the latter in the majority; Jews and Protestants and Catholics; those welcoming slave ownership and abolitionists; many who supported the Union in Civil War times and—mostly—those who sided with the Confederacy.

During the American Civil War, German immigration ceased, then doubled after the conflict. Later arrivals did not settle in the Texas Hill Country or much in the German Belt. They chose the cities. In 1880 the census declared that San Antonio's population was one-third German.

But by 1900 German emigration slowed. Then, two world wars brought immigration to an end except postwar migration to cities. Prejudice generated by the world wars also worked against the use of spoken German in Texas, including German-language publication. More general causes—depopulation of rural areas and inevitable intermarriage—reduced German prominence.

After 1900 Texas Germans entered virtually every occupation in the state, and some names, such as rancher Robert J. Kleberg and Admiral Chester W. Nimitz, became very well known indeed.

A central part of Texas's Hill Country is still called the "German Hill Country." German food, family customs, and remnants of architecture and of the language remain.

Easter Fires

German customs, brought to Texas intentionally or intuitively, are numerous. One of the oldest, perhaps brought by settlers from Westphalia and Lower Saxony, is the custom of lighting bonfires on hilltops as part of a Spring festival.

This distantly pre-Christian custom is as delightfully pagan as decorated eggs and trees (later becoming "Easter" eggs and "Christmas" trees). Not only does German influence seem responsible for Christmas trees, but these settlers brought the fires.

Today, in Fredericksburg (and formerly, infrequently, in places such as Boerne) Easter church bells ring Saturday evening, many town lights are darkened, and more than 20 fires blaze from surrounding hills. Of course, the occasion has become a popular modern festival, but the fires illuminate an old local story.

As told in Fredericksburg, the fires date from a first Easter observance in 1847, when Comanche Indians lit signal fires around the German settlement as the colonial leader, John O. Meusebach, negotiated a treaty. In this story, the signal fires scared the children, who were assured by their parents that the flares were nothing more than fires over which the Easter rabbit was cooking eggs for decoration.

Meusebach's treaty, however, took place a month before Easter in 1847, so the story cannot be quite as it is told.

Perhaps the Easter rabbit needed an advance start in the new land. Perhaps the Comanches did use this not very common way of communication. Perhaps. But more than likely, settlers from southern Germany would not have known the custom of the fires and may have been scared by Westphalians out having fun.

In whatever version, the story is a good one. And however altered, those old fires of the European Spring still burn in Texas.

Chester W. Nimitz (in his U.S. Naval Academy uniform) with his family

The German-English School on South Alamo Street in San Antonio, c. 1895

The Latin Settlements

Most German immigrants to Texas were called "solid peasant stock," and most were exactly that. The first generation largely farmed, but very quickly some of the first and second arrivals were entering all professions.

A few German settlers, however—idealists rather than farmers—established the so-called "Latin Settlements" in Texas. Five in number, the settlements were founded by highly educated Germans, almost all younger men, who departed a troubled mid-19th century Europe. The 1848 revolution in Germany, an example of failure in its object to shift political and economic power, did add to the reasons for emigration and not necessarily for farmers. Some who would not otherwise see opportunity in frontier farming became exiles.

Latin, until three generations ago, was an academically common language necessary for higher learning and a sign of a proper and worthwhile education. But where major human goals are to bring in a crop or earn a profit, Latin is no necessity.

A small number, therefore, of university students and young professionals who found Europe politically hostile tried their hand on the Texas frontier. Millheim in Austin County, Latium in Washington County, Bettina in Llano County, and Sisterdale and Tusculum in Kendall County were founded.

Bettina is one of the most interesting examples of the effort. Nearly 40 young men, calling themselves *Die Vierziger* (both in reference to their number and to the troubled 1840s in Europe), subcontracted settlement rights from the German immigration society that managed much land beyond New Braunfels and Fredericksburg. Nearly all of these men were—or had just been—students at Giessen and Heidelberg. Experience they had in architecture, languages, medicine, education, mathematics, and law; they had *no* experience in farming. Yet their ideal was to establish a communistic agricultural community on the Llano River which would soon attract 200 German families.

The settlement was named Bettina after Bettina von Arnim, a German writer and an "ideal woman" to the young men.

Arriving in 1847, the group built two notable structures: a thatched storage shed and an shingled adobe house. In the next year they managed a corn crop of nearly 200 bushels. By late summer—and with a Texas winter on the imagined horizon—the colonial effort failed.

Some of the young men reportedly worked hard; some of them apparently sat in the shade of oak trees philosophizing and thinking of pleasant student days. The latter were accused of trying to live according to the perilous maxim *Ede, bibe, post mortem nulla voluptas*, as it was later quoted ("Eat and drink, for after death there is no pleasure"). As readers of Horace's *Odes*, they probably remembered *Carpe diem, quam minimum credula postero* ("Enjoy today; have little trust in tomorrow").

Whatever was on their minds, a knowledge of Latin was neither sufficient nor necessary for frontier agricultural success. Preparing for tomorrow *was* necessary.

Almost all of the men drifted away, some to other areas of German settlement, some to a more urban setting. The name Bettina only remains on a few older maps.

And what was true of Bettina was almost true of the other Latin Settlements. The little communities provided newcomers—who were often successful in their academic fields—to places like Houston and San Antonio. Sisterdale, Latium, and Millheim still exist with populations of about 100; Tusculum provided an impetus for present-day Boerne. All the areas are rich with memories.

In one of the old locations—which cannot be revealed—people have seen and heard a ghost who, beyond doubt, dates back to settlement days. Ghosts are not unusual in Texas, but this one speaks a fluent, academic Latin.

Gathering of the original New Braunfels settlers in front of the Sophienburg

San Antonio Schützenverein (shooting club), c. 1890

Rancher Johanna Wilhelm (inset);
the Great Barn on the Wilhelm Ranch, 1904—Mrs. Wilhelm is in the buggy (left),
and Clara Wilhelm is in the sidesaddle (third from right).

The Wendish Texans

Reverend Johann Kilian and his daughter

The Wends of Texas represent a small Slavic group of people who have never had an independent nation and who have undergone a double assimilation in Texas.

Known as Sorbs or Lusatian Serbs, Wends have lived in Lusatia, Eastern Germany, as a recognizable group from the Middle Ages until today. Just before 1850 some Wendish families emigrated to Australia; then, hearing of German settlement in Texas, a few Wends came to Austin County. In 1853 about 35 Wends entered Galveston to settle in New Ulm and Industry.

The only larger group of Wends ever to leave Europe was a congregation of Lutherans led by Johann Kilian. This group, decimated by cholera in Liverpool and yellow fever in Galveston, eventually settled in present Lee County, where Johann Dube and Carl Lehmann had purchased a league of land. Johann Kilian's two-room house served as the church, and the settlers initially lived in dugouts. By 1860 a community named Serbin warranted a post office. The settlement grew until 1871, when a new railroad turned Giddings into the population center for the area.

Life for the first generation was hard, and the Wends were conservative. Dancing and secular music were considered inappropriate activities; the main job in life was making a living, not preserving tradition. Since they came from Germany, most Wends considered it natural to live among already-established Germans in Texas.

Even in Europe, the Wends were largely "Germanized" by the 19th century. In Texas they became more so; Wendish families living in German settlement areas were quickly assimilated. Those Wends who spoke only Sorbian learned German as their second language, then English. By World War I most of the Wends in the state had adopted German. The Giddings *Deutsches Volksblatt* contained a few columns of Wendish for a number of years, then shifted entirely to German.

Most Texas Wends simply consider themselves German, but in the Serbin area, considerable identity has been maintained through a revival of interest in earlier Wendish characteristics.

St. Paul's Lutheran Church, Serbin

Wedding reception of Emma Jurk and Bernhard Joseph Schmidt, Warda, 1907

Some individuals today maintain that no intermarriage has taken place in their families since the main Wendish arrival in 1854. But for the most part, intermarriage and an acceptance of German, then Anglo, customs has meant a thorough acculturation for most families.

The Texas Wendish Heritage Society was founded in 1971, when the group began its annual participation in the Texas Folklife Festival of the Institute of Texan Cultures, and the membership maintains a Wendish museum at Serbin. The group has revived interest in European costume, foods, and crafts and is attempting to collect, translate, and publish early Wendish documents. Many were lost during the first years in Texas.

The community at Serbin holds an annual Wendish Fest and extends a welcome, *Witajcže K'nam*, to visitors. During the affair church services are conducted in German and English, a Czech band may play, and corn-shucking contests are held. Some of the local descendants dress in European Wendish costume.

The Wends of Texas represent one of the strongest examples of cultural revival by later generations.

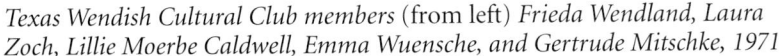

Texas Wendish Cultural Club members (from left) *Frieda Wendland, Laura Zoch, Lillie Moerbe Caldwell, Emma Wuensche, and Gertrude Mitschke, 1971*

Emma Jurk and Bernhard Joseph Schmidt, 1907—Formerly associated with Texas Wends is the German Lutheran custom of a black wedding dress. The symbolic color was a reminder of the difficulties, pain, and grief accepted as parts of marriage. In time, the custom changed. Wedding dresses became gray, then white by the turn of the century. Marriage may have become no easier, but later generations of women did not want that reminder on their wedding day.

The Czech Texans

Frances Drozd Mendl in an embroidered Czech outfit, c. 1933

Czech presence in Texas has been clear and profound. For this group of Slavic peoples, language preservation marked, at one time, their ethnicity. Other traditions are obvious—foods and music among them—and for these people, farming was not just an occupation but a philosophic life goal.

Many Czechs arriving from 1850 to the First World War considered the establishment of a self-sufficient farm as the most desirable, proper, creative way of life, not simply a way to make a living. On the ideal Czech farm, the family raised one cash crop (cotton or corn in Texas) and produced everything else they needed. The cash crop bought anything that could not be grown or made at home.

Before a Czech wedding could take place, the prospective couple had to own or rent land on which to farm. And nearly all the farms created a prosperous life for the first two generations. The Czech way of life is also described in another word: work.

The Czechs, arriving long before the establishment of Czechoslovakia in 1918, were a Slavic people of Bohemia, Moravia, and Silesia. Texas became home for many of the Moravians, and the Moravian dialects became Texas Czech. Perhaps because of their many European years of domination by other peoples, Czechs arrived in Texas with a love of democracy and individuality.

Immigrants settled in some 250 Czech communities mostly on the Blackland Prairie. Lavaca and Fayette Counties were heavily settled, with small centers appearing in Brazos, Burleson, and Williamson Counties. North of these areas, Czechs settled in Bell, McLennon, Ellis, Hill, and Kaufman Counties. Texas's Coastal Plain, below and within the German Belt, attracted hundreds of families.

Fayetteville, originally a German settlement, became Czech by the 20th century. The city is often called the "cradle of Czech settlement in Texas." Many Czech families, even though not settling nearby, passed through on their way up-country.

For the Czechs, the retention of language, in addition to the establishment of farms, was key to their culture. Czech language classes were started everywhere there were Czechs. School lessons

Baca's Family Band, Fayetteville, 1907

in Czech were held at Cat Spring by 1855, and Josef Mašik opened classes at Wesley in 1859. By 1870 the school at Praha combined Czech with English instruction. And the younger generations advocated the study of the language in universities.

This emphasis led to a widespread organization of Czech-language newspapers. Some 33 publications were established, and, even though the use of Czech dramatically declined, two papers still existed in the 1990's: *Našinec* at Granger and *Hospodár* at West. Other newspapers still contain Czech columns.

Such a strong retention of language undoubtedly has much to do with the oral literatures—folktales, sayings, and songs—that remain in Czech areas.

Czech communities, supported by strong fraternal and insurance organizations, still embrace wedding ceremonies, foods, music, and recent costume reproductions that are unmistakably European.

Czech organizations were not all fraternal. The *Cechie* supported the teaching of advanced Czech as well as literature and history. In 1915 the organization was instrumental in influencing the University of Texas at Austin to establish a Chair of Slavic Languages. One of the most interesting organizations is the *Sokol* ("falcon"), which advocates the equal development of both mind and body. Essentially classical Greek in concept, the organization was founded in Prague in 1862, making its way to Texas by 1908. *Sokol* groups engage in gymnastics, dancing, singing, art, and literature.

Today, nearly 170,000 Czech descendants maintain several community museums and a number of festivals in the state. Most Czechs have now left the family farm for urban occupations, as did most people in Texas, but many smaller settlements remain on the map and in people's hearts.

Sokol meet in Granger

Wedding of Charles H. and Bertha Knesek Cmajdalka in Fayetteville with the Fayetteville City Band

The Polish Texans

Reverend Leopold Moczygemba

Immaculate Conception of the Blessed Virgin Mary Church, Panna Maria

Polish Texans were, for many years, one of the most isolated, tradition-preserving, conservative, and rural ethnic groups in the state.

Individuals were in Texas as early as 1818, when several Polish soldiers who had served in Napoleon's defeated armies joined the French settlement of Champ d'Asile on Texas's Trinity River. The Spanish saw the colony as an incursion, and the settlement was shortly disbanded.

But Champ d'Asile was somewhat typical of Polish fortune. From the end of the 18th century until World War I, Poland was conquered, overrun, partitioned between stronger neighbors, and suppressed as far as national autonomy was concerned. The country endured typhoid and cholera epidemics and floods, such as a combined disaster in 1854 which wiped out food production. In many years, Poland was not a desirable place to be.

At first, individuals, mostly men, left the country as soldiers of fortune or simply wanderers. After the mid-1850s, emigration of Polish families greatly increased. Emigration to Texas, as a group movement, started largely through the efforts of Father Leopold Moczygemba, a Polish Franciscan missionary, who was working in the San Antonio area. He was quickly involved in bringing 100 families from Upper Silesia to Texas.

This group founded the town of Panna Maria in Karnes County on December 24, 1854; the group's first mass was held Christmas morning. The settlement is the oldest permanent Polish colony in the United States and is the location of the first Polish Catholic church and school.

In one year 700 others joined the colony, although most of these people settled at a distance. Later arrivals started or helped settle such towns as Cestohowa, Kosciusko, Polonia, Chappel Hill, and Bryan. Panna Maria itself became a "mother colony," sending people to such centers as White Deer in the Panhandle, San Antonio, Bandera, and McCook in the Rio Grande Valley. New Waverly in Walker County was the first Polish settlement to the east.

The first and part of the second generation of Polish Texans generally remained somewhat isolated in their communities. Their lives centered around the church and rural life. Education—after establishment of St. Joseph's school at Panna Maria—and contact with other communities were considered of secondary importance.

The natural result of this isolation was a preservation of community feeling. A number of fraternal groups and organizations were established in the state, but until the later part of the 20th century, and with the exception of identifiable groups in Bryan, Houston, and San Antonio, Poles lived in rural groups.

Many families spoke Polish at home, but publishing in Polish was not established in Texas, and the language was not generally taught. Only one Polish-language newspaper, *Nowiny Texaskie (Texas News)*, was published in San Antonio from 1913 to 1920.

Today, 250,000 individuals in Texas claim Polish descent, and statewide organizations and festivals mark the fact. Urbanization has caught up with most of these people as it has for nearly all Texans. Today, individuals of Polish descent have entered occupations from the state legislature to banking, from ranching to the priesthood, from engineering to art, from writing to medicine.

Soldiers from Poland

Coming from a partitioned country, Polish men often entered military service in other countries such as France or Spain as a way of making a living and perhaps a fortune. From time to time, Texas was appropriate.

At the upstart French Champ d'Asile, the Napoleonic artilleryman Constantin Malczewski helped plan the fortifications that were never to be used except in later French fiction. He became a general of artillery in the Mexican army. Captain Joseph Alexander Czyczeryn was a member of Dr. Long's filibustering expedition, which entered Spanish Texas with revolutionary hopes in 1821.

After the unsuccessful uprising against Russia in 1830, many Poles left for anywhere. Some of these found the Texas Revolution timely and sufficiently dangerous. Michael Debricki, a major in Poland, was an engineer at Goliad. Also with Fannin's artillery were the brothers Francis and Adolph Petrussewicz and John Kornicky. The artillery commander killed at Coleto was Francis Petrussewicz. All others were executed with Fannin.

Felix Wardzinski was a San Jacinto survivor who became a landowner in Harris County and a veteran of the Mexican War. An enlistee, he fought with Texas volunteers at the Battle of Monterrey.

Private Kaminski, losing his first name to bad record keeping, was in the Texan army in 1840. He died opposing Comanches during the Council House fight in San Antonio.

And the presence of military men and women of Polish descent extends into contemporary times in great numbers.

The John Gawlik house in Panna Maria, built in 1858, a good example of Upper Silesian folk architecture in Texas

Wedding of Pauline Tudyk and Thomas Katzmarek in St. Hedwig, 1894

The Italian Texans

General Vicente Filisola

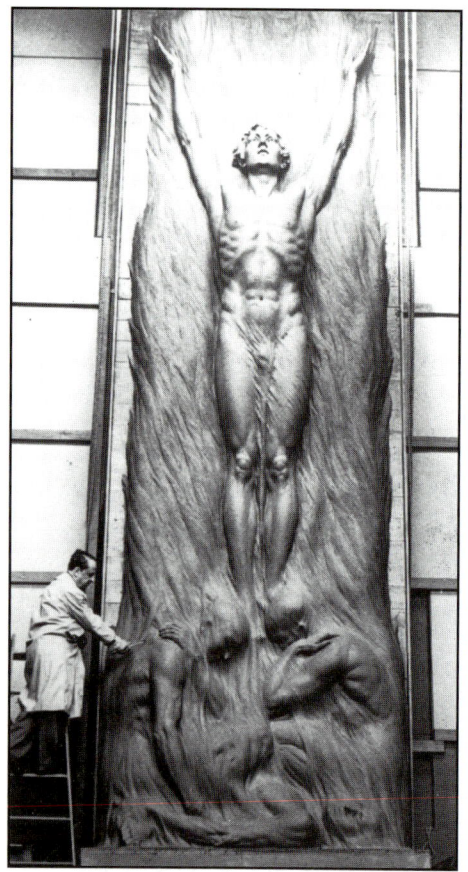

Prolific sculptor Pompeo Coppini (here working on the Alamo Cenotaph) contributed greatly to Texas.

Until the mid-19th century, Italians coming to the Texas area were adventurers, explorers, or soldiers.

Italian explorers, from the 15th and 16th centuries, were well known indeed, but none came in the service of an Italian city or province. In the mid-16th century—and for many years before and after—the Italian peninsula was a mass of republics, city-states, kingdoms, and duchies. Some enjoyed fair economic independence, but none could mount New World exploration like Spain and Portugal. Thus, adventurous Italian soldiers and sailors took employment elsewhere.

According to some documentation, Amerigo Vespucci saw the coast of future Texas in 1497 while determining for Ferdinand of Aragon whether the new lands of Columbus were Asia—or an unknown continent. Vespucci did not command the voyage but was official observer for the king on this and three later voyages more of confirmation than exploration.

A number of the soldiers with Vásquez de Coronado's expedition as it crossed Texas's high plains were Italian. Later, Henri de Tonti, serving his commander and friend Sieur de La Salle, entered Texas in 1686 and 1689 searching for La Salle's settlement and made records of his visit. Tonti, born near Rome, was a resourceful and colorful Italian, known in the New World for his artificial hand made from copper and his presence up and down the Mississippi.

Later Italians came to trade and stay. Vicente Micheli was an early Texas settler in the East Texas fur trade at Nacogdoches in 1793. Entering ranching and horse trading, Micheli moved to San Antonio after 1806. As owner of Rancho de San Francisco and a mercantile store, he called himself the "Merchant of Venice."

During the Texas Revolution Giuseppe Cassini (called José Cassiano in San Antonio) provided the rebellious Texans with food from his store. For this he had to flee his home, but after the revolution he returned to San Antonio and became a land dealer with extensive holdings.

General Vicente Filisola was second in command to General López de Santa Anna during the revolution. Filisola proved a durable soldier, escaping attempts to make him a scapegoat for Mexico's loss of Texas. He remained in military life through the Mexican War. Stephen F. Austin, who met Filisola in 1833 before decisive hostilities, declared him a "blunt, honest, candid and prompt soldier . . . he is the friend of the farming and agricultural interests—a decided enemy of smugglers and lawyers." General Filisola remained loyal to Mexico during the revolution, but others, such as Prospero Bernardi, fought on the other side with Sam Houston at San Jacinto.

In 1870 only 186 Italians were listed on Texas's census records. But by 1920 the number was over 8,000. Significant Italian emigration was a part of the 1880–1920 surge from southern and eastern Europe. Many Italians in these decades, moving away from economic depression and warfare in Europe, headed for the coasts of the Gulf of Mexico. Texas received a substantial share.

And when they came in these years, the Italians most often settled with their geographic compatriots. Piedmontese settled in Montague County. Individuals from Venice and Modena joined Piedmontese in the coal mines of Thurber. Lombardy provided hands for the New York, Texas and Mexican Railway between Victoria and Rosenberg. And Sicilians settled in Galveston County and up the Brazos River valley.

Urban communities followed in Galveston, Houston, and San Antonio. As with other immigrant groups, many of the first arrivals, mostly younger men, settled to establish families.

Josephine Lucchese, internationally renowned coloratura soprano and daughter of Sam Lucchese, San Antonio bootmaker, began her singing career in 1922 and retired in 1970.

La Tribuna Italiana

For some 50 years, *La Tribuna Italiana*, founded by Charles Saverio Papa of Sicily, was the banner of Italian culture in Texas, Oklahoma, and Louisiana.

Papa arrived in Dallas in 1908, calling the city "Venice" because of unusual floods that year. He operated a barbershop for some five years, then—without a press or money—decided to start a newspaper. What he did have were four words for the masthead: *Justice, Freedom, Opportunity, America*. He soon had an Italian printer, Louis Adin, who could run a linotype machine. Papa could sell advertising.

The Italian-language newspaper proved a success and supported communities in three states.

In 1940, when Benito Mussolini declared war against the Allies, *La Tribuna Italiana* changed its name to *The Texas Tribune* and its language to English.

The paper survived Adin's retirement and Papa's accidental death, until 1962. In a last editorial, logical reasons were given for ceasing publication. The claim was made that the paper had always supported the advancement of Italian communities. It had also worked for the "amalgamation of our people into the whole American society." With that accomplished, publication could cease.

Italian Club picnic at the mining town of Thurber, late 1800s

The Japanese Texans

The story of Japanese arrivals to Texas is one of the most varied in terms of reasons or motives. Japanese Texans came by choice or invitation, as relocated businesspeople, through government order, and as forced prisoners.

In 1902, under government pressure created through overpopulation in Japan, Sadatsuchi Uchida toured the Gulf Coast with an eye to emigration possibilities. Many Texas businessmen appreciated the visit, indicated that Japanese farmers would be welcome, and invited settlement efforts.

Some of the immediate leaders were prominent. Seito Saibara, a lawyer, businessman, former university president in Kyoto, and former member of the Japanese parliament, came to Webster near Houston in 1902. Businessman Kichimatsu Kishi settled in Terry near Beaumont. Both brought families as well as single men and successfully set up rice farms. These efforts attracted others, and, although the rice market failed 15 years later, many stayed, some changing their investment to truck farming.

For a short time, some of these settlers wore traditional Japanese field dress and practiced their native religions. Most kept a low profile, deliberately adopting Western clothing and local beliefs.

Another small wave of Japanese families arrived in Texas from the West Coast, driven away by anti-Japanese feelings there. They settled mostly in Cameron and Hidalgo Counties in the lower Rio Grande Valley, while a few chose El Paso and Bexar Counties.

These arrivals were welcomed, but by 1920 the American Legion post in Harlingen told Japanese immigrants to stay away, and the following year the Texas legislature passed a law prohibiting the owning or even leasing of land by foreign-born Japanese.

World War II brought a strong, illogical, but certainly understandable reaction against Japanese immigration and also against individuals of Japanese descent living in the United States. The Bexar County Japanese were particularly noticeable in a military city, and the Jingu family, who had helped create the Japanese Tea Garden for San Antonio, were forced to leave. The garden was hastily renamed the Chinese Tea Garden.

During World War II nearly 6,000 "alien" Japanese arrived as prisoners, called internees, in three federal camps in Texas: Seagoville, Kenedy, and Crystal City. Many of these Japanese were former West Coast residents, and at the close of the camps, a few made Texas home. Some stayed because their properties on the West Coast had been confiscated and sold.

After 1950 the Japanese population turned urban, and assimilation increased. Many of the individuals coming to Texas were "war brides," Japanese women who had married American servicemen. For a time, Japanese women in Texas greatly outnumbered the men, and the women themselves formed clubs to teach each other how to deal with a very different land.

The ban on Japanese naturalization ended in 1952, and immigration laws were relaxed; but in general, the Japanese did not target Texas as a new home.

Some of the Kimi Jingu family posing at the Japanese Tea Garden, where they lived and sold refreshments to visitors at San Antonio's Brackenridge Park, 1937

Rice workers on a farm near the Texas coast wearing traditional Japanese rice-straw hats, 1905

Seito Saibara's new (1904) house on his rice farm near Webster

Many recent arrivals have been sent to Texas by Japanese firms establishing branch operations in urban centers. In 1997 in Houston more than 100 Japanese companies were represented, and persons working for these firms outnumbered Japanese Texans descended from earlier settlers.

Today, the second and third generations of Japanese Texans—the *nisei* and *sansei*—are concentrated in Houston, Dallas, and San Antonio.

Federal High School graduates, 1945, in the Crystal City Internment Camp

The Chinese Texans

Column of Chinese and Mexicans following the Pershing expedition out of Mexico, January 28, 1917

Wedding portrait of Mrs. Mow Wah Chin

The Chinese, initially arriving in Texas as laborers and facing decades of exclusion laws, were often seen by others as stereotypical Orientals: railroad laborers in unusual dress who ate strange food, set up instant laundries, and associated with peculiar gods. Because of the times, much of the image was accurate.

The first Chinese, seeking jobs that would allow them to return to China with money, were single men. Most in Texas worked on railroad construction crews. Some 250 Chinese were on the Houston and Texas Central construction in 1870. A few stayed in Robertson County at the end of the railroad work as cotton sharecroppers. Other than a few individuals, these were the only rural Texas Chinese, then or now.

A second group, nearly 3,000 from the West Coast, worked on the Southern Pacific construction as the line moved east from El Paso. Blasting powder and desert heat were not the only perilous aspects of this job. Judge Roy Bean, the "Law West of the Pecos," ruled at least once that there was "no law against killing a Chinaman." And members of a surveying crew, including 11 Chinese, were killed near Eagle Pass on the last day of 1881 by Apaches. Or so the raiders were identified. After 1883 some workers settled in El Paso County, but by that year further Chinese emigration to the United States was virtually halted. Anti-Chinese sentiment, much originating on the West Coast, created exclusion laws that allowed very few individuals to enter the country.

Only in 1917 was an exception made. U.S. General John J. Pershing had been ordered into Mexico to destroy the forces of Francisco "Pancho" Villa, who had raided into the United States. Pershing's unsuccessful pursuit was supported by hundreds of Chinese families in northern Mexico. Perhaps hoping to be allowed into the United States, they provided the expeditionary army with food and supplies in an otherwise hostile countryside. More than 500 families followed Pershing out of Mexico and were given special permission by the U.S. government to stay, on provisional terms. Some 400 of these families were allowed to settle in San Antonio to become the first Chinese community in the state.

The first arrivals, unable (and, in any case, not allowed) to bring families (with the exception of "Pershing's Chinese") intended to make money and leave. Most did. They were laborers who took work where few others would, such as on railroad crews, or where their presence would offer no economic threat, such as sharecropping or running a laundry. They were mainly single men, mostly southern Chinese who spoke Cantonese.

When China became a World War II ally, the feeling in the United States changed to some degree, and the exclusion act was repealed in 1943.

After World War II northern Chinese, Mandarin speakers and often from well-educated upper-economic classes, came to Texas. Many specialized in medicine, sciences, or engineering. These later arrivals could and did establish the traditional extended families—very patriarchal—and lived together in enough numbers to celebrate Oriental holidays and traditions.

Of more importance, later generations maintained the traditional family and merchant associations. A few organizations based on province of origin were established. All of these supported Chinese families in economic terms. This generation claims very few individuals ever listed on welfare rolls.

Emphasizing education, the Chinese made several efforts at establishing Chinese schools, where the language and some history were taught. San Antonio's school was operated from about 1922 to 1947. Ending for a time, it was revived in 1971. Another school has operated in Houston most years since 1970.

Many present-day Chinese Texans are Christian, and many customs have yielded to Western tradition. Still, their Lunar New Year is commonly celebrated, and most people remember that firecrackers (even on the 4th of July) are a popular Chinese contribution to life in the United States.

Traditions and Legends

Chinese culture is one of the oldest in the modern world. Individuals who read Chinese can understand a language that has remained remarkably stable in written form for thousands of years. And the earliest Chinese history includes legends and metaphoric language that bother few Oriental scholars but do puzzle Western historians.

For centuries the Chinese—in a wonderful irony—have regarded North America as the "Far East," just as earlier Europeans called China the "Far East."

And the Chinese "Far East" has been known to them for more than 3,000 years. Whether this knowledge is based on travel across the Pacific or is just a good guess remains speculation. But in the past two decades, Western historians have realized that early China was not the isolated country it became in the 19th century.

Government documents from China in the sixth century, in part rejected as fiction by many Western historians, record the journey of a Buddhist priest to the Far East. Hwui Shan returned from somewhere to tell a tale, and the bow and arrow may have appeared in North America just about the time of his journey.

Even more strange, the oldest geography of China, finished at least 2,000 years ago, includes land traverses in this Far East. One of the outlined journeys curiously matches West Texas. No hard evidence exists. Only written records were created. And few people really think a Chinese explorer walked across trans-Pecos Texas more than 20 centuries ago.

Or did he?

Lion dancers, San Antonio, 1983

The Dutch Texans

Except for a few troubled decades, the Dutch have had little reason to make Texas their home. Yet certain individuals, and one colonial effort, made huge differences to the state.

Probably the most influential was Phillip Hendrick Nering Bögel, the self-proclaimed Baron de Bastrop, who was directly responsible for Anglo-American settlement in the Mexican state. An arrival in Texas after 1795, the baron made friends easily and was soon a confidante of many Spanish, then Mexican, officials.

Befriending both Moses Austin and Stephen F. Austin, Bastrop convinced the Mexican government to admit the first colony of Anglos.

Other Dutch individuals were similarly notable in the Texas story. David Levi Kokernot was a Dutch Jew born in Amsterdam but raised in New Orleans. Kokernot became a warrant officer in the U.S. Revenue Cutter Service and first saw Texas as a shipwreck survivor at the Sabine River.

Kokernot apparently liked the rather vacant land. By 1832 he had settled with his family at Anahuac and enthusiastically fought in the Texas Revolution. After the siege of Béxar, Kokernot became a friend of Sam Houston and carried out special and secret missions for the general. When the general became President Houston, Kokernot was given command of a ranger company.

In 1853 Kokernot moved west and, during the Civil War, served first in Louisiana, then, at 60, as a home guard volunteer in Texas. Although a soldier all his life, after the Civil War he consolidated some of his West Texas land holdings. These grew into a half-million-acre ranch in Jeff Davis, Pecos, and Brewster Counties.

Many Dutch coming to Texas were opposed to slavery, did not sympathize with the Civil War, or liked a good fight less than Kokernot. Few came; few stayed. But by the latter 19th century, Holland was overcrowded and in an economic depression.

In 1895 the Port Arthur Land Company was formed by Dutch investors. Some 66,000 acres of land in southeastern Texas were offered for sale in Holland at $8 an acre. Advertisements showed the land as a paradise, but most of the favorable land in the area had been taken. What was for sale was low-lying marsh. Still, the land company did build the Orange Hotel, named for Holland's royal family and painted a bright orange color.

Immigrants came, most were grateful for the hotel, and many stayed.

The first was George Rienstra, who, in 1897, chose what he thought was the best available land. Joined by his sister, Fanny, and brother, Dan, he was soon raising rice. Others followed, and the settlement was named Nederland.

Even some South Africans came to the colony. All of the African Boers (the Dutch farmers) did not find the continent profitable. Some heard about Texas and tried their luck in a move. Gerrit Trewey, after trying both Canada and South Africa, came to Texas's Nederland colony. Finding the place acceptable, Trewey journeyed to Holland to marry Machteldje de Jong, and the two spent their honeymoon aboard ship bound for Texas. William de

From a monument in the town of Bastrop

The Baron de Bastrop

The most controversial of Dutch immigrants, Phillip Hendrick Nering Bögel, was possibly the most influential and perhaps the first. He left his homeland, wife, and children, having embezzled the results of his work as a tax collector.

In Spanish Louisiana by 1795, he had enough money to introduce himself as Felipe Enrique Neri, Baron de Bastrop, to the highest aristocratic circle and was soon engaged in a series of land deals in Louisiana and the U.S. He made more than one fortune but lost them all.

About 1810, nearly broke but with a good change of clothes and the requisite languages, he traveled to San Antonio and, by conversation and appearance alone, was soon made second *alcalde* (a mayor pro tem) of the city. He presented himself as a loyal Spanish subject who had opposed the sale of the Louisiana territory by France to the United States. France had ceded the lands west of the Mississippi to Spain in 1762, but by 1800 King Charles of Spain had been forced to give the lands to Napoleon Bonaparte and France. Napoleon, needing money and tired of New World involvement, sold the land to the U.S. In such a place, just *who* was Spanish was sometimes in doubt.

Nelly Rienstra in 1903, before she married Klaas Koelemay

Vries, a friend of Trewey, came in 1911, worked for a time on the Galveston seawall, then moved to Nederland.

The colony only enjoyed moderate progress until 1901 when the discovery of oil, then the largest known field in the western United States, gave the colony a sound economic future.

The pattern of settlement was typical. And Nederland exists today, between Port Arthur and Beaumont.

The Baron de Bastrop's story was believed and, within only months, his advice was sought as far as Mexico City concerning the dangerous United Statesians. Yet the baron seems to have been responsible for Anglo settlement in Spanish and Mexican Texas.

Twenty years before his arrival in Texas, Bögel had shared the hospitality of a roadhouse in then-Spanish Missouri with a lead miner named Moses Austin. And in San Antonio de Béxar, in 1820, he recognized Austin, who had just been rejected in his request to bring in settlers. In fact, he had been ordered out of Texas.

The baron asked Austin to stay with him for several days, under the pretext of sickness, while the request was reworded. Austin, like Bastrop, quickly became a loyal Spanish citizen who was outraged at the transfer of the Louisiana territory. Austin, like Bastrop, only desired to live under Spanish rule but, a bit unlike the baron, wanted to bring in several hundred like-minded and loyal Spanish citizens.

This time, permission was granted. After all, the baron had used nearly the same line.

Even after the death of Moses and a change of governments—Stephen F. Austin had taken over his father's work, and New Spain had become Mexico—the baron continued to help. He was influential in renewing the agreement.

After the establishment of Austin's colony, Bastrop was named commissioner of colonization for the colony. He helped issue land titles and became Austin's confidante. Further, he was elected to the Legislature of Coahuila y Tejas and served until his death in 1827. The self-appointed baron never made much money in Texas, but he became an Anglo friend. If Stephen F. Austin is the "father of Anglo Texas," the Dutch con man Bögel is certainly the godfather.

At Bastrop's death, legislative members paid for his funeral. His will left land claims to his wife and children in Holland; years later, these records finally revealed his true identity.

Dutch settlers in Nederland photographed after the harvest

Martin Koelemay harvesting rice, Pine Island Bayou, 1902

The Belgian Texans

The story of Belgians in Texas is diverse but hardly fragmented. Belgium has consistently sent priests, builders, scientists, musicians, professionals, craftspeople, and farmers out into the world. Although never in great immigrant numbers, Belgians and Belgian influence have been notable in Texas.

As part of La Salle's French colonial efforts in 1685, three priests born in Hainaut arrived: Zenobius Membre, Maximus le Clerq, and Anastasius Douay. Membre and le Clerq died in Texas during the Indian attack on Fort St. Louis, but Douay lived to tell Europe his story and the story of La Salle's death.

Juan Banul, a master blacksmith, was born in Brussels but when Belgium was under Spanish rule. Perhaps having a love of frontiers, Banul came to New Spain and moved north to San Antonio de Béxar by 1719.

Banul accompanied the Marqués de Aguayo to East Texas on an expedition to build missions and presidios and stayed until 1723. Back in San Antonio, he did much of the ironwork at the missions of San Antonio de Valero and San José. In 1730 Banul and Maria Adriana García, a Flemish widow, were married. They lived at Valero, later called the Alamo, where Banul ran the blacksmith shop and sawmill.

Much later, in the 1850s, a Belgian stonemason, Theodore Vander Straten, helped repair the Alamo walls so the building could be occupied by the U.S. Army. Army designers, not interested in restoration, added the now-famous curve to the church façade.

Some Belgians arrived with strange stories. Anton Diedrick, walking in Antwerp in the 1840s, came across a murder in progress. The killers turned on him, but instead of murdering their witness, they kidnapped him and literally sold him as an impressed seaman. A virtual prisoner once aboard ship, Diedrick finally escaped in Galveston just in time for the Mexican War.

Speaking only Flemish, he was warmly welcomed by two recruiters for the U.S. Army. They asked his name, but when he began replying in some detail, he was stopped. "Ah, he's Dutch all over," one of the recruiters said. "We'll call him that."

So it was that Anton Dutchallover served in the war, survived, and lost the "all" from the middle of his new name.

Becoming a frontier scout, Dutchover joined Big Foot Wallace as shotgun rider on the infrequent San Antonio-El Paso runs in the 1850s. West Texas was well known for hostile climates, renegade Indians, and bandits, but Dutchover liked it.

He operated a sheep ranch at Limpia Canyon and supplied soldiers at nearby Fort Davis with food. Dutchover remained at the fort when Federal troops departed at the start of the Civil War and was left fully in charge when the occupying Confederates decided to leave. Dutchover, his family, and four civilians hid during a successful Apache attack on the fort and maintained their home until 1867, when Federal troops reoccupied Fort Davis and made further Indian raids impossible.

Dutchover descendants still live in the area.

Anton (Diedrick) Dutchover and family

A contemporary of Diedrick, but very well known, was Jean-Charles Houzeau, a famed Belgian astronomer and naturalist. The scientist came to New Orleans after being removed from the Belgian Royal Observatory for "outspoken political views." In Texas by 1858, he first worked as a surveyor, then moved to Uvalde and organized early scientific expeditions.

But the astronomer's outspokenness remained. An abolitionist, he aided the escape of notable unionists from San Antonio but soon had to flee, disguised as a Mexican laborer, into Mexico.

Later in New Orleans, when the city had been taken by Federal forces, he ran a Union newspaper, then for eight years lived in Jamaica. Finally, having kept his European contacts, he was reinstated as director of the Royal Observatory in Brussels.

In December of 1882, however, Houzeau could not resist a return trip to Texas. He led a scientific expedition to San Antonio to observe a locally visible transit of Venus across the face of the sun—in those days a method of measuring time and gravity.

A few Belgians moved into South Texas after 1867 and the fall of Maximilian's Mexican empire. Maximilian, anointed emperor of Mexico by the French, was an unlikely ruler. His wife, Carlota, was Belgian, and a good number of her countrymen had followed the puppet emperor to Mexico. After Maximilian's execution, many Belgians decided on the Rio Grande valley as home.

Belgians moved to Galveston and Houston, and some were farmers, but San Antonio became Texas's primary area of Belgian settlement. Although entering many fields of endeavor—Belgians were cooks and bakers, candle and soap makers, restaurateurs and musicians—most in the San Antonio settlement were farmers.

From the last of the 19th century, several Belgian families and descendants founded the famous vegetable farms in western San Antonio. Men such as Van de Walle, van Daele, Persyn, and Baeten made year-round vegetable growing a successful business. The Belgians raised common crops and introduced new ones, including cauliflower and kohlrabi. Today, harvests range from flowers to picante sauce.

And the Belgians observed the "Kermess," a national fall harvest festival held in mid-August—and in mid-November, if the harvest was good. They also celebrated Belgian independence day on July 21. The Belgium Inn, the Belgian Village, and the Flanders Inn, among several other places, provided the settings for many a gathering, traditional or impromptu. And until recent years, the Belgian sport of bolling was played. A version of the game is still demonstrated annually at the Texas Folklife Festival.

Vegetables ready to go to market in San Antonio, c. 1908—(from left) *Prosper Vervaet; his wife, Emma; Delphina Bauwens; her son, Aviel; and his wife, Mary*

Bolling at the Belgian Village in San Antonio, c. 1935—(from left) *Maurice Verstuyft, Cyril Verstuyft, August Stevens, Frank Bache, and Rene Persyn*

Octave Van de Walle's farm on Zarzamora Street, San Antonio, c. 1908

The Greek Texans

The Very Reverend Theoclitos Triantafilides, first priest of the Serbian, Greek, and Russian Eastern Orthodox church of SS. Constantine and Helena, Galveston

Bishop John of Thermon (holding Bible) at his Orthodox Holy Ordination ceremony (the first to be held in Texas) in the Annunciation Greek Orthodox Cathedral, Houston, 1970

Greeks and people of Greek heritage came to the Americas and Texas mostly between 1890 and 1920. Greece has been a colonizing country for some 2,500 years; thus, some Greeks came from Greece itself, others from satellite colonies in the Middle East. Many Greek colonials were expelled from Turkey during warfare. In Greece economic depression at the turn of the century, overpopulation, and—not incidentally—social customs such as an expensive dowry system that had to accompany marriage, drove many individuals to seek fortunes elsewhere.

Greek emigrants to Texas went directly into cities. Here, the typical single man would work in a low-paying job until he had earned the money to open his own business. If he met with success, and most did, this prosperity led to a trip home for a marriage and a quick return to Texas.

But the first to arrive were rather different adventurers. Captain Nicholas, who never admitted another name, was a young pirate who sailed the schooner *Arabella* as part of Jean Lafitte's buccaneer fleet. Coming into his share of luck, Nicholas tried to settle down by buying himself a Karankawa bride (for 10 pounds of sugar and an undisclosed quantity of rum), lost her in a storm, sailed with Lafitte off Yucatán, survived yellow fever, escaped wrecks, and returned to Galveston on board a Texas Navy ship in 1842. The apparently indestructible captain finally did settle down in Galveston, living both by his wits as a storyteller in the port city and as a farmer. Just a few days before his 100th birthday, still going strong, Nicholas died in the Galveston storm of 1900.

Some individuals of Greek descent came early to Texas on very different business. Colonel Francisco Garay, with General Urrea during the Texas Revolution, managed to save a few men from the Palm Sunday massacre at Goliad. Born of Greek parents, Garay had served the Mexican Republic as consul at Gibraltar and attaché in London before joining the army and finding himself in Texas as part of a very bloody revolution.

Later Greeks, seeing Texas as a home, stayed and formed small communities. Galveston, as Texas's leading seaport before the rise of Houston, was a lure to fishermen, sailors, and merchants. There, joining with Orthodox Syrians, Serbians, and Russians, the Greeks helped build the SS. Constantine and Helen Orthodox Church, where the first priest, the Greek Theoclitos Triantafilides, conducted services in Greek, Russian, and Serbian.

Some individuals worked their way to Galveston as seamen, leaving ship there for other lives; others abandoned railroad work for urban Texas settings; many lived elsewhere before moving on; and a few had heard about Texas and took it as their first choice. In an era when women did not travel singly or alone, most women were brought as brides.

Typically individualistic as Greeks are, Faithon P. Lucas summarized immigrant feeling after, as a cafe owner in Dallas, he was called a "damn foreigner."

"Friend," Lucas remarked calmly, "I am ashamed that I was not born here, but I came as quickly as I could." This might have been remark enough, but holding his accuser's eye, he continued, "And I have done my best to be worthy of America. But I am just as ashamed as your grandfather was when he arrived."

Greek urban communities typically centered around the church or social societies. By the 1940s communities existed in all of Texas's larger cities—San Antonio, Dallas, Houston, Galveston—and also in Waco, Austin, Wichita Falls, El Paso, Port Arthur, and San Angelo.

March 25, Greek Independence Day, has been observed officially in Texas since the governor's proclamation in 1943 of "Greek Independence in Texas." The day is marked in homes, churches, and community centers with a feast, costumed dances, religious services, and speeches.

The church is the focus for most of the Greek festival days, which include Christmas Eve midnight services; gifts on New Year's (St. Basil's Day, although this is yielding to today's commercial Christmas); the blessing of the waters at port cities on Epiphany; somber Good Friday processions; and the feast of Easter Sunday with its notable breads, pastries, cheeses, and, in former years, roast lamb and costumed dancing.

And the Greek wedding may still extend in excess of the hour needed for the exchange of ceremony, although the duration is shorter than the former 10-day celebration. Also, to nearly everyone's delight, the dowry system has been mostly abandoned.

Ancient Greeks contributed much to Western culture—structures of literature and government, music and philosophy, science and drama; modern Greeks have helped construct Texas.

Dancers celebrating the 50th anniversary of the first Annunciation Greek Orthodox Church, Houston, 1965

The Garden Fruit Store, San Antonio, belonging to Elias Varessis (Pappa Louis)

The Filipino Texans

Most of the Filipinos in Texas are comparatively recent arrivals. Strong economic and political ties with the Spanish empire from the 16th to the 19th centuries brought few known individuals to the Americas, but United States control in the early 20th century was responsible for Filipino settlement in every metropolitan area in the state.

Considering the Spanish trade with the Philippines—the Manila galleons operated between Acapulco and Manila from 1565 to 1815—travelers from the islands may have been in Mexico after the mid-16th century.

The first Filipino known by name in Texas arrived in 1822. Francisco Flores from Cebu, a cabin boy on a freighter, decided to make Port Isabel his home. Some time later he owned a fishing business with two schooners. At 40 Flores married Augustina Gonzales and moved the family and business to Rockport. He witnessed a long span of Texas history, dying in 1917 at the age of 108.

The Spanish-American War, at the end of the century, was responsible for the first substantial entry of Filipinos to Texas. The United States, acquiring the Philippines from Spain by military conquest—and for a payment of $20 million for Spanish improvements—maintained a substantial number of servicemen in the islands. Military rule lasted until 1907, after which a civil government was instituted. A large number of Filipinos were hired as servants, mainly by military officers, and when the servicemen returned to the United States, some employees followed. Many came to San Antonio, which has always been a military city.

A few Filipinos who had moved to other parts of the United States chose Texas as a home because of the climate.

During World War II many Filipino men joined the United States armed forces. At the independence of the islands, granted by the U.S. in 1946, these men could become citizens because of their service. Many did, some continuing their military careers. And language was never a problem. Filipino and English were official languages, and Spanish was still present in the homeland.

After 1945 the United States became attractive to Filipino professionals: doctors, engineers, nurses, bankers, architects, accountants, pharmacists... Some Texas locations were favorable for those entering with work visas. Other arrivals to Texas were second-generation, born in the United States.

Colonel Melecio Montesclaros (right) *accepting the flag of Ft. Sam Houston at the change of command ceremonies, 1973*

Captain Anita Perdiz Satterly, c. 1983

Dr. Anatolio B. Cruz Jr.

Captain Anita Perdiz Satterly, born in the U.S., became a nurse and administrator for the Public Health Service in Galveston and Nassau Bay. Melody de Guzman Barsales served for 18 years on the heart-transplant team of Dr. Michael DeBakey of Houston. Lucy Naguit Pendon, born in Bataan during World War II, became a hospital administrator in Freeport. Dr. Anatolio B. Cruz Jr., a surgical specialist from Rizal, a province of Luzon, advanced to the academic rank of full professor of surgery at the University of Texas Health Science Center in San Antonio.

Houston became home to about 2,000 Filipino nurses, San Antonio to somewhat fewer. Today, some 20,000 Filipinos live in Texas. Until the last two decades, most were foreign-born. These are urban settlers who are succeeding in preserving a significant number of Filipino customs.

A Cultural Mix

Filipino society for centuries has been a mix of native, invited, and imposed influences. This remains the case in Texas today.

In the Philippines Spanish conquest added Catholic festivals and the observances of saints' days to the regional celebrations of the 7,100 islands making up the archipelago. United States control, from 1898 to 1946, and continuing influence after independence, added Protestant beliefs (in small quantity) and North American music, holidays, and dress.

Even the traditional formal male shirt, the *barong tagalog*, is an imposed dress. In the 19th century rich Filipinos began wearing Western frock coats. As a sign of servitude, the Spanish forbade them to tuck in their shirttails. The Filipinos obeyed but produced shirts of beautiful embroidery and wore them with pride. Today, the shirt is a modern national costume.

Filipinos thus wear a mixture of regional and Western dress and celebrate Catholic and Protestant feasts and national observances. The 4th of July is now Philippine-American Friendship Day.

In Texas several Filipino performing arts groups replicate and modernize traditional dances. Earlier Filipinos were known for dances of harvest, battle, death, marriage, birth—all the seasons and passages of life. Much of their original costume and ritual combined Hindu, Arabic, Malayan, Spanish, and "American" sources as well as native forms.

The modern dances have distinctly new costumes influenced by centuries-old design; the dances are altered to fit the modern world but are related to older dances performed in the Philippines.

And most Filipino homes in Texas contain art and crafts as much a part of life as memory.

Filipino Community float in a Fiesta San Antonio parade

Filipino dance group at the Texas Folklife Festival, San Antonio

The French Texans

René-Robert Cavelier, Sieur de La Salle

Henri Castro

Although a French flag of some sort is represented in "six flags over Texas" displays, France never—in any sense of political control—flew a flag over Texas and never gave her own citizens strong reasons for emigration.

However, René-Robert Cavelier, Sieur de La Salle, *did* make one foray west of the drainage of the Mississippi, and General Charles Lallemand *did* lead a short-lived military colony into East Texas.

France, in the New World, was more interested in trade than settlement and was often distracted by continental European problems. The nation was neither equipped for colonial ventures nor had that much interest in the western Gulf of Mexico.

Nevertheless, in 1685 the young Sieur de La Salle landed at Matagorda Bay, Texas, some 600 miles west of his target: the Mississippi River. The few colonists he brought were to found a colony at the mouth of the Mississippi, to which France did have a claim, and thus tie down France's claims that, for a time, stretched from Canada to the Gulf—in theory.

Encountering storms and perhaps suffering bad navigation, the ships found the Spanish coast. Navigation in those days could determine, with an exactness of perhaps 30 miles on a good day, position north and south. But the day was not good, and the northern shore of the Gulf of Mexico stretches more east and west. In those days, east and west positions on a rotating globe were hard to determine.

Thus, scholars still argue whether the French landfall was a mistake or a deliberate measure to test Spain. In any case, Sieur de La Salle's group built a stockade named Fort St. Louis. In a short time, the fort was ransacked by natives and the colonists killed or dispersed. The effort, which Spain soon knew about, had the effect of drawing Spanish exploration and mission-founding efforts into the eastern parts of the province.

More than a century later, in 1818, General Lallemand led a group of Emperor Napoleon's former officers and soldiers into Spanish lands near present Liberty. The area, nearly vacant then, seemed a likely place for the group. Baron Charles François Antoine Lallemand, general in the service of and friend to the emperor, could have made his motives clear but did not. The baron claimed the settlement was agricultural; rumor called it a military colony from which an effort could be launched to rescue Napoleon and reinstate his empire. But the skills of soldiers proved

Castroville in the 1880s, the first St. Louis Catholic Church (c. 1845) at far left; the second St. Louis Church in center foreground; and the most recent St. Louis Church, built in 1870, on the right

inadequate for a frontier, and the Spanish army threatened an assault. The group struck camp, never to return, but, as with La Salle, still roused Spain to secure the Texas borderland. In fact, the attention called to the area by the "colony"—called Champ d'Asile—resulted in the Sabine River being declared the border of Louisiana and Texas.

But the Republic of Texas, some years later, was faced with the problems of a population too small for a nation, so in 1841 laws were established allowing for colonization efforts. This was the empresario system, begun for Texas by Spain, under which a grant was made to an organizer, the empresario, who would bring in colonists for a large land bonus.

In 1847 Henri Castro was one of several who took advantage of the law. Castro was a fairly wealthy French banker who had a taste for adventure. In two years his efforts resulted in the founding of Castroville west of San Antonio, and in three years more than 2,000 French Alsatians had made it their home.

Castroville, unlike other French efforts, remains.

Also after 1841 French missionaries were directly responsible for the revitalization of the Catholic Church in Texas, which had been virtually rejected after the Texas Revolution as being simply a part of Mexican rule. This effort established schools and hospitals across the state.

A good number of French Acadians also made Texas their home but only after a couple of moves. A settlement of Canadian French, living in a Nova Scotia colony named Acadia, were expelled by the British in 1775. Many came to French Louisiana and became U.S. citizens when the young country bought Louisiana. They were known as Acadians, or "Cadians," then "Cajuns."

Generations later, especially during and between the two world wars of the 20th century, many came to Texas on the wave of wartime prosperity. The war years were, in general, boom years for Texas rice production, oil refining, explosives manufacturing, and ship building in the Houston-Golden Triangle part of the state.

In particular, the Golden Triangle (Orange, Port Arthur, and Beaumont) is a modern home for the Cajun language, a French-based creole laced with idioms from English, German, Spanish, American Indian, and black dialects and languages. Cajun cuisine is likewise extraordinary.

Today, Texas organizations such as the Alliance Française celebrate Bastille Day, preserve spoken French and French foods, and serve as reminders of the French influence in Texas as well.

Giraud's French Gothic

François Giraud, born in South Carolina of French parents, studied engineering in Paris, then decided on Texas as a home. In 1848 he became the first surveyor for the city of San Antonio. In 1854 he convinced city officials to set aside San Pedro Springs as a park, now the second-oldest city park in the United States.

Giraud redefined the boundaries and structures of the Spanish missions and established his name as an architect by designing the buildings for the old Ursuline Academy (today's Southwest Craft Center) and the main buildings of St. Mary's University.

One of his most interesting design accomplishments is the French Gothic cathedral of San Fernando, a building enclosing the old walls of the original Spanish parish church. The cathedral opened formally in 1873, while Giraud was serving as mayor of San Antonio.

San Antonio's Ursuline Academy designed by Giraud, now the Southwest Craft Center

Benjamin Foulois with the No. 1 Wright Pusher airplane, Eagle Pass, 1911—He soloed in a Wright Type B at Ft. Sam Houston in 1910 and by 1915 commanded the newly formed First Aero Squadron, which was to develop into the world's greatest air force. He was the first American to fly in combat (during Pershing's expedition against Pancho Villa in Mexico) and was chief of the Army Air Corps from 1931 to 1935.

The Lebanese and Syrian Texans

Annie Swia Casseb with baby George and Solomon (Sr.), c. 1900—Solomon established the first supermarket (c. 1923) in San Antonio.

Texans descended from those who came from the present-day areas of Lebanon and Syria number fewer than 30,000, yet they have established some of the most lasting communities.

Perhaps the first Syrian to come to Texas was Hadji Ali, born Orthodox and raised Moslem, who landed in Indianola in 1856. Among his shipmates were 33 camels. The Syrian was a caravaneer for the United States Army, then experimenting with the use of camels for transportation. Hadji Ali stayed in Texas only a short time but did pick up a new name: Hi Jolly. He moved on to Arizona, where he lived for more than 50 years. He is buried under a small stone pyramid with an iron camel on top.

Most Arabic-speaking emigrants came between 1880 and World War I. Many of the first arrivals were Christians, who abandoned their homelands because of religious persecution. Few of the earlier individuals were Moslem, but after 1945 hundreds of Moslems came as a result of military conflict in the Middle East.

The first individuals and families either entered Texas through Mexico or came after entering the United States at New York. Originally from the Ottoman Empire's provinces, the immigrants were simply called "Syrians" until Lebanon became a nation in 1919. Referring to the history of the eastern Mediterranean, many of them appropriately consider themselves of Phoenician descent.

Urban in settlement pattern, the first generation of mostly young men were traveling salesmen or operated tiny businesses. Some individuals dreamed of enjoying a few prosperous years in Texas, then returning home. Few did. The next arrivals established themselves as retail merchants, educators, lawyers, oil producers, and manufacturers. And they established extended families.

The Lebanese and Syrians were typical in acculturation, but many families maintained Arabic as a home language, while

Solomon and George Casseb's produce store, San Antonio, 1915

stressing the need to handle English well. Most preserved their cultural heritage in terms of food, music, and literature.

Individuals often maintain close family ties to Lebanon and Syria, and visits to the homeland are frequent in comparison to some cultural groups.

Most families belong to the Lebanese Maronite Rite Catholic Church, although Orthodox churches exist in several cities including Beaumont, El Paso, Austin, and Houston.

Community groups often formed close-knit organizations. Many of these were church-oriented; others were formed by individual families. Today, the Southern Federation of Syrian Lebanese American Clubs has many Texas members. This nonpolitical federation stresses both Americanization and the preservation of ethnic pride. The organization, often working through local clubs, sponsors economic aid, scholarships, and literary and civic awards.

Houston community groups are well known for retaining Arabic as a family language and maintaining cultural traditions at gatherings called *sahrias*. These are held in many communities by families, clubs, and churches, and feature traditional foods, dances, music, and costume.

In San Antonio many families are Maronites, an Eastern Rite of the Catholic Church in which the mass is conducted partly in Arabic. The church remains the community center, and the group spirit is strong enough to support periodic special events during the year with Arabic music, dancing, and food.

The most well-known names in the state have become legendary: George Kadane and Michel T. Halbouty in oil exploration and production; J.M. Haggar, clothing manufacturer and noted philanthropist; Najeeb E. Halaby, former president and chief executive officer of Pan American World Airlines and operator of an international law firm, whose daughter, Lisa, is married to King Hussein of Jordan and is now titled Queen Noor al Hussein; Dr. Michael DeBakey, the internationally known cardiovascular surgeon; and lyric soprano Helen Donath.

The Leon Curry family, c. 1900—Son Joseph Curry invented and manufactured machinery used in processing Mexican food, and his brother, Peter Michael Curry, was a military officer in World War II, then practiced law in San Antonio, becoming a district judge in 1967 and serving until his retirement in 1992.

St. Michael's Syrian Orthodox Church, Beaumont, c. 1936

The Tejanos

A Spanish priest celebrating mass for Indians, c. 1629

16th century method for loading horses on ships— During transit they were supported by slings.

European Spaniards and their descendants were the dominant peoples of Texas for more than three centuries—from the beginning of the 16th century until well into the 19th. The Spanish changed New World history, native peoples, and even the land far more than others.

The Spanish came to Mexico and Texas as conquerors—soldiers, settlers, and priests. Other than exploitation of natural resources (gold, silver, timber, fibers) and human resources (Indian slaves), the Spanish goals were to impose religious and social orders on the natives and to set up a civilization matching what had been accomplished in Europe.

Texas remained a frontier under the rule of the Spanish, but the conquerors were relatively successful, considering their small numbers.

To some degree, the Spaniards were changed by the land and the people they found. Spanish religion and temperament condoned (and even encouraged) mixed marriages. Spanish law generally extended social rights to all free or freed people, whatever the mix of European or Indian or African, although government employment of any rank was reserved to those of "pure" Spanish blood.

In the New World the Spanish Indians, the *mestizos*, quickly became numerous and important. People in Texas were called, and called themselves, Spaniards, Mexicans, Tejanos, Texas Mexicans, and, in recent years, Hispanics, Latinos, Mexican Texans, Mexicanos, Mexican Americans, la Raza, Chicanos, and, again, Tejanos. One single name has never been accepted by those of Spanish-Mexican-Indian descent, and some names have been socially or politically rejected by nearly all of such descent.

But by whatever name, the first Spaniards, later to be Mexicans, came to change things...and did.

Into a land that was, in anthropological terms, in a Stone Age, the Spanish brought European horses and armor and firearms, the ranching and farming traditions of Spain, legal and religious systems of tremendous power, architecture, printing, a common language and literature, European crafts and arts, as well as cows, sheep, donkeys, goats, chickens, and pigs, and grapes, peaches, and other crops.

Things would never be the same again.

The Spanish discovery of Texas and the first good map of the coast are attributed to Alonso Álvarez de Piñeda, who skirted the Gulf in 1519. Alvar Núñez Cabeza de Vaca was shipwrecked on the coast of Texas in 1528. He and three companions survived to tell and write about the Texas region.

The Spanish searched Texas for gold and silver such as they had found in Mexico and Peru. The name "Florida" promised beauty, and "New Philippines" hinted at just as much treasure as in the East Indies. But the Spanish were profoundly disappointed by the lack of treasure in Texas. Nevertheless, partially in response to politics, they extended the mission and presidio system northward and formed colonization schemes. Few succeeded for long.

Spanish efforts resulted in only three permanent settlements in the province of Texas: San Antonio (1718), La Bahía (Goliad, 1749), and Nacogdoches (1779). Los Adaes, in present Louisiana, was the provincial capital for a time, and Laredo (1775) was originally in Coahuila. Present trans-Pecos Texas now includes early settlements near El Paso dating from 1682, but at the time, that area was in the province of Nueva Viscaya.

Thus, the Spanish government moved several thousand settlers and soldiers and missionaries to the few villas and a central ranching region stretching from San Antonio de Béxar to Goliad.

Still, the Spanish were few. Settlement in Texas was not popular, and the road from the interior of Mexico was a hard one. The missions, villas, and presidios were largely self-sufficient in terms of agricultural products but were dependent on imported manufactured goods—weapons, cloth, gunpowder, sugars, and wine—although the settlers attempted the manufacture of all.

Texas became known as a cattle-raising province. A few big ranches and the missions, the major landowners at the time, raised large and profitable herds. Trail drives were organized in the 1770s as *vaqueros* moved cattle to Mexico and east to Louisiana. The latter route was in support of the Spanish on the Gulf Coast, who found themselves on the unlikely side of Anglo settlers in the War of Independence against Britain.

Frontier areas, when not very well supported by a central government months away, are ripe for revolution, and by 1800 the Spanish empire was tottering. Citizens of mixed blood were beginning to do more than just resent the rule of the "pure" Spaniard.

Conditions made Texas a battlefield. In 1811 revolution against Spain erupted as Captain Juan Bautista de las Casas convinced the presidial troops at Béxar to overthrow the local government. This effort lasted but a few weeks. The next year José Gutiérrez de Lara entered Texas with some Anglo-American backing and a small revolutionary army, and, for less than a year, Texas had an independent government. But Spain's royalists once again took over and ruled until 1821, when Mexico itself, including Texas, threw off the leadership of the ageing empire.

As a Mexican state, Coahuila y Tejas had a short but significant life. Even as a Spanish province, most of the people in Texas were natives of Mexico, if not born in the province itself. They were the ones who had built the villas and ranches, the schools and churches. They had no more tendency to look to central Mexico than they had to Spain. They were of independent mind. Although the word was not used in colonial times, they were *Tejanos*.

Mexico and Spain had created a society of Tejanos in Texas that was adaptable and productive. Yet this frontier culture was no match for the future competition with Anglo-Americans, who came from the United States in greater numbers and possessed a better technology in terms of communications and weaponry. Within two years of Mexico's independence from Spain, significant numbers of Anglos were allowed to enter Texas. Once the door was opened, it could not be closed.

Mexico established a congenial constitution in 1824, but a few years later Antonio López de Santa Anna rejected it in his rise to power. Some Tejanos stood with Anglo Texans in opposing the dictator. (The majority of Tejanos simply tried to keep out of harm's way.) Soon, another revolution was in full cry.

18th century vaquero herding cattle on a Spanish ranch

Misión San José, San Antonio, 1860s

Juan Martín de Veramendi's palace when he was governor of Coahuila y Tejas in the early 1830s, Soledad Street, San Antonio, c. 1870

General Antonio López de Santa Anna, 1837

José Antonio Navarro

Juan Nepomuceno Seguín

As Santa Anna's armies initially overran Texas, they were often brutal in their treatment of Tejanos, even though they were their countrymen. Tejanos died at the Alamo and served at San Jacinto. But after the successful Texas Revolution, many Anglos hated everything Mexican and made no distinction between Tejanos and Mexican nationals. Many Tejano families left for Mexico after the revolution of 1836.

Exceptions there were. José Antonio Navarro served in the congress of the republic and was a senator in the first two state legislatures. Antonio Menchaca was a mayor pro tem of San Antonio. Francisco Ruiz served as the first Bexar senator to the Texas congress. Juan Seguín led a cavalry unit protecting Sam Houston's army and reentered San Antonio after the retreat of the Mexican army. He gave the funeral oration for the slain Alamo defenders.

But the political dance of the United States and the Republic of Texas called for a merger. And with the merger came new conflict. The war of 1846–1848 between Mexico and the United States, enthusiastically supported by the new State of Texas, established expanded borders for Texas that the republic could not have defended and widened the gap of hate between the people of Mexican descent and the Anglo-Americans.

Many Tejanos left for Mexico as the best chance, if not a good one. For some 60 years immigration from Mexico nearly ceased. The new state became literally Anglo in influence, head count, culture, and language.

Some Tejanos stayed in spite of prejudice, theft of their land, and relegation to "second-class citizen" status. Descendants of earlier arrivals managed a life in San Antonio and El Paso, and families stayed on the South Texas ranchlands they called home. But they were few and no longer in economic control.

Yet, from the turn of the 20th century, Mexico was a land of revolution and agricultural disaster. The inability of many people, landowners and laborers alike, to make a decent living caused hundreds of thousands of Mexican citizens to enter the United States. In the next 60 years, because they swelled the ranks of necessary, cheap labor, they were welcome. Many Europeans came in the early part of the century for the same reasons.

And the Texas-Mexico border is easy to cross. By the mid-20th century, one out of every five Texans was of Mexican descent—the new Tejanos. By 1990 the count was one in four. And by 2030, demographers estimate, the Anglo and "Hispanic" populations will be about equal—each at some 42 percent of the total number of Texas citizens.

As in nearly every century of Texas history, the European-Spanish-Mexican-Tejano heritage is easy to see. Texas is, after all, not simply an Anglo United States' state, but also a former state of Mexico and a former Spanish province. This shows not only in the people but in foods, dress, music, customs, laws, language, architecture, beliefs, and religions as well.

Spain brought Europe to Texas, and Mexico brought the New World—the result was the Tejano.

Chili stand on Military Plaza, San Antonio, c. 1885

Activist Emma Tenayuca in front of San Antonio's City Hall leading a demonstration, c. 1937

Charro Days parade, Brownsville, 1970s

ITC Product Information

To Learn More about Texas History and Cultures...

Thank you for purchasing *Texans One and All* on the ethnic and cultural groups represented on the ITC Exhibit Floor. With informative, enlightening prose and fascinating historical photographs and illustrations, John L. Davis has captured the essence of the people of Texas.

But there is so much more to learn! The Institute presents historical and cultural information in a variety of ways, and we invite you to peruse the list below for just a sample of our other products and services. Whether through publications and audiovisuals, traveling exhibits and photographic collections, teacher training and the Internet, or special events and exhibits, ITC remains steadfast in its mission of symbolizing the state's strength in diversity. We believe we have a strong message to give, and our work will not be complete until we begin to make a difference in the lives of all Texans and, indeed, people everywhere.

Sample Products Available through the ITC Catalog of Products and Services

Call (800) 776-7651 for a free catalog.

Audiovisuals
Contemporary Indians of Texas Video Series
Workin' from Can't to Can't: African-American Cowboys in Texas Video
"Many Tricksters" Audiocassette Tape

Posters
Texas Folklife Festival Commemorative Poster Series
"Texas Post Office Murals of the New Deal" Posters
Early Texas Indian Mural Poster Series

Publications
Ethnic Book Series: *The English Texans, The German Texans, The Hungarian Texans,*
  The Irish Texans, The Japanese Texans, The Polish Texans, and *The Swedish Texans,*
  as well as pamphlets on a number of other ethnic groups
Texans: A Story of Texan Cultures for Young People
The Melting Pot Cookbook

Traveling Exhibits
The Impact of World War II on Texans at Home
"Like a Double-Edged Sword": The Black Civil Rights Movement in Texas
Texas Women: A Celebration of History
Mexican Folk Toys
Ranch Women: Roles, Images, Possibilities

Traveling Trunks
Cowboys and Cattle Drives
The Other Cowboys
Texas Indians Who Lived in Houses
One-Room Schoolhouse

The ITC Store

Major Special Events
The Texas Children's Festival, April
The Texas Folklife Festival, August

The Internet
www.texancultures.utsa.edu

The ITC Library
Noncirculating historical research materials
More than three million photographic images

The ITC Store
The Institute gift shop is filled with a delightful assortment of both ethnic and Texana books and merchandise from publishers and vendors all over the world selected to please every pocketbook. The possibilities are beautifully eclectic: from French Limoges plates and African baskets to a variety of items from Texas artisans. Store hours correspond to ITC hours of operation.

Other ITC Books by John L. Davis

*Explorations in Texas:
   Ancient and Otherwise,
      With Thoughts on the Nature of Evidence*

The Texas Rangers: Images and Incidents

Photo Credits

All prints are from the collections of The University of Texas Institute of Texan Cultures at San Antonio [ITC], courtesy of the following lenders. Credits for photos positioned from top to bottom are separated by semicolons, from left to right by dashes. Uncredited photos are staff productions of the Institute of Texan Cultures.

Page vi	St. Stanislaus Museum, Bandera.
Page viii	Zintgraff Collection, ITC, courtesy John and Dela White.
Page xiv	*San Antonio Light* Collection, ITC.
Page 2	Sandra Hodsdon Carr, San Antonio; Alice Sackett, San Antonio.
Page 3	Library of Congress, Washington, D.C.; Western History Collections, University of Oklahoma, Norman.
Page 4	Allen Richards, San Antonio; Charles G. Downing, Eagle Pass.
Page 5	Dorothy Shill, Livingston; Calleros Estate, El Paso.
Page 6	Texas Memorial Museum, University of Texas at Austin; Mrs. Artie Fultz Davis, Navasota.
Page 7	Winston Farber, Houston; San Antonio Conservation Society, San Antonio.
Page 8	*San Antonio Express-News*, San Antonio.
Page 9	Erna L. Boggus, Yancey; Houston Metropolitan Research Center, Houston Public Library.
Page 10	Marcella Giles Booth, San Antonio.
Page 11	*San Angelo Standard Times,* San Angelo—Edith Anson Boulware, San Angelo; Erwin Smith Collection, Library of Congress, Washington, D.C.
Page 12	Peter Bógati, Budapest, Hungary; Fred Petmecky, Buchanan Dam.
Page 13	Bernice Casey, Waco; Milton Varga, San Antonio.
Page 14	General Thomas J. Green, *Journal of the Texian Expedition against Mier* (New York: Harper, 1845).
Page 15	Southwest Collection, Texas Tech University; ITC; Archives Division, Texas State Library, Austin.
Page 16	Celeste Hopkins Brown, Victoria; Archives Division, Texas State Library, Austin.
Page 17	Sisters of the Holy Spirit, San Antonio; Linda Salyers, Corpus Christi.
Page 18	Hansen Collection, Ella Hansen, Danevang; Verner A. Petersen, Danevang.
Page 19	Archives Division, Texas State Library, Austin; Verner A. Petersen, Danevang.
Page 20	R.W. Reierson, Houston; Mrs. William E. Warenskjold, Cleburne.
Page 21	Mr. and Mrs. Clarence Colwick, Clifton; Mrs. O'Belle Harris, Grand Prairie.
Page 22	Olga Pearson, Hutto.
Page 23	August Anderson ["Q-r"], *Hyphenated; or, The Life Story of S.M. Swenson* (Austin, n.p., 1916)—Center for American History, University of Texas at Austin; New Sweden Lutheran Church, New Sweden.
Page 24	Mrs. Charles C. Bush, San Antonio.
Page 25	Texas Southern University, Houston; Annie R. Lee, San Antonio.
Page 26	Melvin M. Sance Jr., San Antonio; Daniel Webster Wallace Estate, Colorado City.
Page 27	John Wildenthal Family, Cotulla; Private Collection.
Page 28	Mrs. Rosella H. Werlin, Houston; Temple B'nai Israel, Galveston.
Page 29	Susan Furman, San Antonio, taken by photographer Brad Townsend, San Antonio; Mr. and Mrs. L.H. Golden, Corsicana; Center for American History, University of Texas at Austin (Negative Number CN 09526).
Page 30	Hermann Hospital, Houston; Mrs. Charles Hetherington, Dallas.
Page 31	Mrs. Arthur Fehr, Austin; ITC, courtesy Mrs. Zachary T. Scott, Austin.
Page 32	Private Collection; Maryann Heimsath, Fayetteville.
Page 33	Pioneer Memorial Museum, Fredericksburg; Witte Museum, San Antonio.
Page 34	Frontier Times Museum, Bandera.
Page 35	*San Antonio Light* Collection, ITC; Heirs of John F. Wilhelm, Menard; Heirs of John F. Wilhelm, Menard.
Page 36	Mrs. Carl Blasig, Giddings; Private Collection.

Page 37	Grace Helen Walther Walker, Seguin; Concordia Lutheran College Library, Austin; ITC.
Page 38	James W. Mendl, Bryan; Gil Baca, Houston.
Page 39	S.P.J.S.T. Supreme Lodge, Temple; Fayetteville Area Heritage Museum, Fayetteville.
Page 40	Sisters of Divine Providence, *Our Polish Pioneers 1855-1936* (San Antonio, 1936); Catholic Archives, San Antonio.
Page 41	T. Lindsay Baker, Canyon; Mr. and Mrs. Emil Mikolayczk, Adkins.
Page 42	Chapultepec Castle, Mexico City, D.F.; Coppini Academy, San Antonio.
Page 43	Florentine Donato, San Antonio; Texas Pacific Oil Company, Dallas.
Page 44	*San Antonio Light* Collection, ITC.
Page 45	May, Julia, and Nina Onishi, Islington, Massachusetts; May, Julia, and Nina Onishi, Islington, Massachusetts; R.C. Tate, Crystal City.
Page 46	Library of Congress, Washington, D.C.; Rose Wong, Austin.
Page 47	*San Antonio Express-News* Collection, ITC.
Page 48	ITC.
Page 49	All three from the Windmill Museum, Nederland.
Page 50	Center for American History, University of Texas at Austin.
Page 51	Mrs. Homer Verstuyft, San Antonio; Mary Ann Scheire, San Antonio; Mary Persyn, San Antonio.
Page 52	SS. Constantine and Helen Serbian Orthodox Church, Galveston; Annunciation Greek Orthodox Cathedral, Houston.
Page 53	*Houston Post*, Houston; Elias Varessis, San Antonio.
Page 54	Col. Melecio J. Montesclaros, San Antonio; Anita P. Satterly, San Antonio—Dr. Anatolio B. Cruz, San Antonio.
Page 55	Virginia Galvan, San Antonio; ITC.
Page 56	Alcee Fortier, *A History of Louisiana* (New York: Manzi, Joyant, 1904); Center for American History, University of Texas at Austin; Esther Nester, D'Hanis.
Page 57	Charles Toudouze, San Antonio; Fort Sam Houston Military Museum, San Antonio.
Page 58	Both from Florence Casseb, San Antonio.
Page 59	Mrs. Ralph N. Karam, San Antonio; Katherine Harris, Houston.
Page 60	Calleros Estate, El Paso; Manuel Alvarez Ossorio y Vega, *Manejo real en que se propone lo que deben saber los cavalleros* (Madrid, 1769).
Page 61	ITC; *San Antonio Light* Collection, ITC; Thomas W. Cutrer, San Antonio.
Page 62	Private Collection; Casa Navarro State Historic Park, San Antonio; Archives Division, Texas State Library.
Page 63	Robert M. Ayres Estate, San Antonio; *San Antonio Light* Collection, ITC; Warren D. Abbott, Austin.

HOUSTON PUBLIC LIBRARY

R01140 59943

```
txr                           T
                              305
                              .90097
                              64
                              D262
DAVIS, JOHN L.
TEXANS ONE AND ALL
```